101 Quick Gifts in Plastic Canvas

the Needlecraft Shop

Table of Contents

Editor	Judy Crow
Product Development Manager	Carolyn Christmas
Assistant Editors	Shirley Patrick
	Jaimie Davenport
Book Design	Greg Smith
Production Artist	Debby Keel
Photography Supervisor	Scott Campbell
Photographer	Andy J. Burnfield
Photo Stylist	Martha Coquat
Photo Assistant	Crystal Key
Chief Executive Officer	John Robinson
Publishing Marketing Director	David McKee
Product Development Director	Vivian Rothe
Publishing Services Manager	Ange Van Arman

Customer Service 1-800-449-0440
Pattern Services (903) 636-5140

CREDITS

Sincerest thanks to all the designers,
manufacturers and other professionals
whose dedication has made this book possible.

Special thanks to
Quebecor Printing Book Group, Kingsport, Tenn.

Library of Congress Cataloging-in-Publication Data
ISBN: 1-57367-120-7
First Printing: 2002
Library of Congress Catalog Card Number: 2002100113
Published and Distributed by
The Needlecraft Shop, Big Sandy, Texas 75755
Printed in the United States of America.

Visit us at
NeedlecraftShop.com

Dear Friends

If your schedule is anything like mine, your feet hit the floor running around 5:30 every morning and you don't stop until 10:00 or 10:30 each night. Every day before I leave for work, I've usually done a load of laundry, made beds, cleaned at least one bathroom and turned on the dishwasher as I race out the door. After work I rush home, prepare a quick meal, spot clean the kitchen, and we're all off to a ballgame, church event or meeting of some sort.

This doesn't leave much time for one of my favorite passions – plastic canvas. I enjoy making everything from home decor to toys and then giving my creations as gifts. I get a real big ego boost when someone says to me "Did you make this? I love it!"

I have found that I can take a small, simple project with me and stitch as I sit in the car or at the game.

101 Quick Gifts is packed full of great tote-along projects. As I thumbed through the pages of this book, I put the name of a special friend or loved one beside certain projects. I can't wait to get started. If I manage my time right, perhaps I can get all 101 made by Christmas!

Happy Stitching,

Judy Crow

Bear Hugs

Designed by Carole Rodgers

Give a hug each time you post a gentle reminder for your family.

SIZE
2½" x 3⅛" [6.4cm x 7.9cm].

MATERIALS
- One 5" [12.7cm] plastic canvas star shape
- Scrap piece of 7-mesh plastic canvas
- 2" [5.1cm] magnetic strip
- Craft glue or glue gun
- Worsted-weight or plastic canvas yarn (for amounts see Color Key).

CUTTING INSTRUCTIONS
A: For Face, cut one according to graph.
B: For Hands, cut two according to graph.
C: For Heart, cut one from star shape according to graph.

STITCHING INSTRUCTIONS:
1: Using colors and stitches indicated, work pieces according to graphs; with maple for Face and with matching colors, overcast edges of pieces.

2: Glue A-C pieces together as shown in photo, forming Bear; glue magnetic strip to wrong side of Bear. Display as desired.

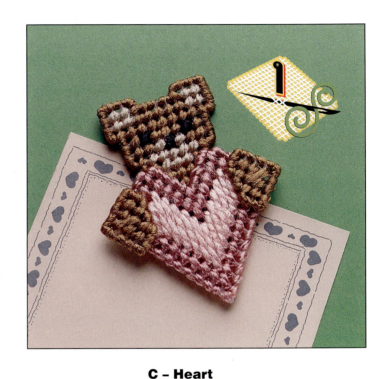

COLOR KEY
Bear Hugs

WORSTED-WEIGHT	
Lavender	2 yds. [1.8m]
Maple	2 yds. [1.8m]
Pink	1 yd. [0.9m]
Sandstone	½ yd. [0.5m]
Black	¼ yd. [0.2m]

A – Face
(10w x 12h-hole piece)
Cut 1 & work.

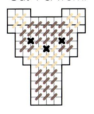

B – Hand
(4w x 4h-hole pieces)
Cut 2 & work.

C – Heart
(5" star)
Cut 1 & work.

Cut away gray area.

Wendy Witch

Designed by Phyllis Dobbs

This cute witch is cooking up some Halloween goodies.

SIZE
3¾" x 4⅝" [9.5cm x 11.7cm]

MATERIALS
- Scrap piece of 7-mesh plastic canvas
- Six-strand embroidery floss (for amount see Color Key).
- Worsted-weight or plastic canvas yarn (for amounts see Color Key).

CUTTING INSTRUCTIONS
For Wendy Witch, cut one according to graph.

STITCHING INSTRUCTIONS:
1: Using colors indicated and continental stitch, work piece according to graph; with matching colors as shown in photo, overcast edges.

2: Using three strands embroidery floss and backstitch, embroider mouth on piece as indicated on graph. Display as desired.

Wendy Witch
(24w x 30h-hole piece)
Cut 1 & work.

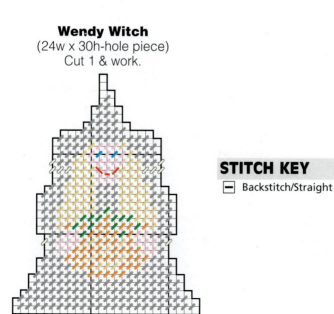

STITCH KEY
- – Backstitch/Straight

COLOR KEY
Wendy Witch

	EMBROIDERY FLOSS	DMC®
🟥	Vy. Dark Rose ¼ yd. [0.2m]	#326

	WORSTED-WEIGHT	NYLON PLUS®
⬛	Black 2 yds. [1.8m]	#02
🟨	Yellow 2 yds. [1.8m]	#26
🟪	Baby Pink 1 yd. [0.9m]	#10
🟧	Tangerine 1 yd. [0.9m]	#15
🟩	Christmas Green ½ yd. [0.5m]	#58
🟦	Royal ½ yd. [0.5m]	#09
⬜	White ¼ yd. [0.2m]	#01

Candy Sleigh

Designed by Mary Henry

Fill this old-fashioned sleigh with treats or pretty ornaments.

SIZE
5¼" x 6½" x 4¼" tall [13.3cm x 16.5cm x 10.8cm].

MATERIALS
- Two sheets of 7-mesh plastic canvas
- 3½" [8.9cm] artificial holly with leaves
- 9" [22.9cm] length of green ³⁄₁₆" [5mm] velvet ribbon
- Two ½" [13mm] gold bells
- 9" x 12" [22.9cm x 30.5cm] sheet of white felt
- Craft glue or glue gun
- Worsted-weight or plastic canvas yarn (for amounts see Color Key on page 8).

CUTTING INSTRUCTIONS
A: For Sleigh Side, cut two according to graph.

B: For Sleigh Bottom, cut one 30w x 59h-holes.

C: For Runner Side Piece, cut two according to graph.

D: For Runner Front Piece, cut one 30w x 5h-holes (no graph).

E: For Runner Back Piece, cut one 30w x 4h-holes (no graph).

F: For Runner Bottom, cut one 30w x 21h-holes (no graph).

G: For Linings, using Sleigh Sides and Bottom as patterns, from felt cut one each ⅛" [3mm] smaller at all edges.

STITCHING INSTRUCTIONS
1: Using white/silver and stitches indicated, work A-C pieces according to graphs; using black and continental stitch, work D-F pieces.

2: With red and embroidery stitches indicated, embroider detail on B as indicated on graph.

3: Whipstitch and assemble A-F pieces according to Sleigh Assembly Diagram on page 8.

4: Tie ribbon into a bow; glue bells to center of bow and bow to front of Sleigh. Glue holly to one side of Sleigh (see photo).

5: Glue G pieces to inside of Sleigh.

A – Sleigh Side
(35w x 23h-hole pieces)
Cut 2. Work 1 & 1 reversed.

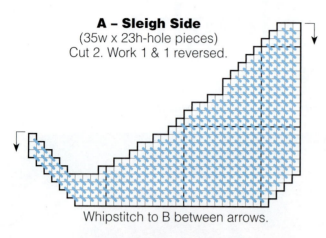

Whipstitch to B between arrows.

C – Runner Side Piece
(33w x 4h-hole pieces)
Cut 2. Work 1 & 1 reversed.

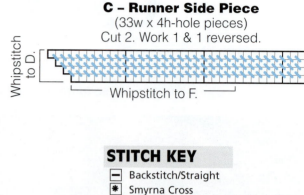

Whipstitch to D.

Whipstitch to F.

STITCH KEY
─	Backstitch/Straight
✳	Smyrna Cross

COLOR KEY
Candy Sleigh

WORSTED-WEIGHT

White/Silver
30 yds. [27.4m]

Red
16 yds. [14.6m]

Black
10 yds. [9.1m]

Sleigh Assembly Diagram
(Pieces are shown in different colors for contrast; gray denotes wrong side.)

Step 1:
With red, whipstitch A & B pieces wrong sides together, forming Sleigh; overcast unfinished edges.

Step 2:
With black, whipstitch D-F pieces together, forming Bottom assembly.

Step 3:
With red, whipstitch C pieces to Bottom assembly; overcast unfinished edges.

Step 4:
Glue Sleigh to Bottom assembly.

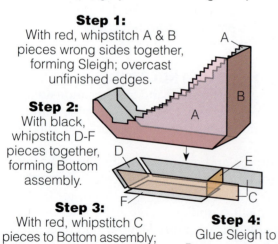

B – Sleigh Bottom
(30w x 59h-hole piece) Cut 1 & work.

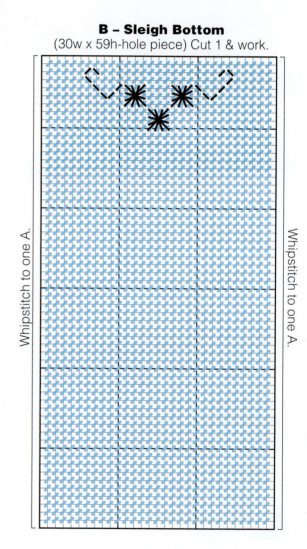

Whipstitch to one A.

Whipstitch to one A.

Inchworm

Designed by Stephen Reedy

Add a measure of whimsy to your fridge or filing cabinet.

SIZE
1½" x 3" [3.8cm x 7.6cm].

MATERIALS
- Scrap piece of 10-mesh plastic canvas
- 1" [2.5cm] magnetic strip
- Six-strand embroidery floss (for amounts see Color Key)
- Sport-weight yarn (for amounts see Color Key).

CUTTING INSTRUCTIONS
For Worm, cut one according to graph.

STITCHING INSTRUCTIONS:
1: Using colors and stitches indicated, work piece according to graph; with matching colors as shown in photo, overcast edges.

2: Using two strands floss and yarn in colors and embroidery stitches indicated, embroider detail on piece as indicated on graph.

3: Glue magnetic strip to wrong side of Worm. Display as desired.

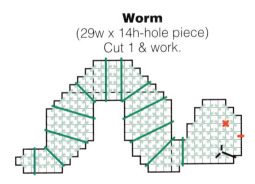

Worm
(29w x 14h-hole piece)
Cut 1 & work.

COLOR KEY
Inchworm

	EMBROIDERY FLOSS	
■ (green)	Green	2 yds. [1.8m]
■ (black)	Black	1 yd. [0.9m]

	SPORT-WEIGHT	
■ (sage)	Sage	3 yds. [2.7m]
■ (red)	Black	½ yd. [0.5m]

STITCH KEY
⊟ Backstitch/Straight

Ghost Fridgies

Designed by Stephen Reedy

Midnight snackers won't be frightened away
by this trio of ghost fridgies.

SIZE
Each is 3" x 3" [7.6cm x 7.6cm].

MATERIALS
- Scrap piece of 10-mesh plastic canvas
- Three 1" [2.5cm] magnetic strips
- Sport-weight yarn (for amounts see Color Key).

CUTTING INSTRUCTIONS
A: For Ghosts #1, cut two according to graph.
B: For Ghost #2, cut one according to graph.

STITCHING INSTRUCTIONS
1: Using colors and stitches indicated, work pieces according to graphs; with white, overcast edges of pieces.

2: Using black and straight stitch, embroider nose on each piece as indicated on graphs.

3: Glue one magnetic strip to wrong side of each Ghost. Display as desired.

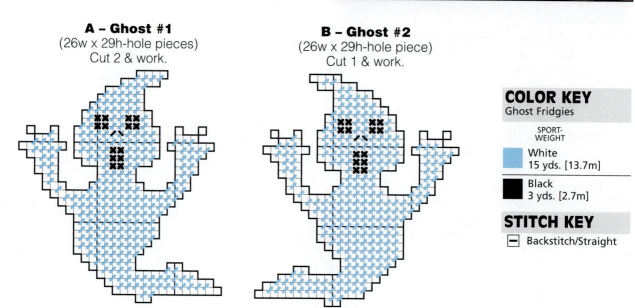

A – Ghost #1
(26w x 29h-hole pieces)
Cut 2 & work.

B – Ghost #2
(26w x 29h-hole piece)
Cut 1 & work.

COLOR KEY
Ghost Fridgies

	SPORT-WEIGHT	
	White	15 yds. [13.7m]
	Black	3 yds. [2.7m]

STITCH KEY
- Backstitch/Straight

Holiday Lights

Designed by Dawn Austin

Light up your holiday celebrations with these clever lights.

SIZE
Each is about 1½" x 2¾" [3.8cm x 7cm], not including embellishments.

MATERIALS
- Scraps of 7-mesh plastic canvas
- One ¾" [19mm] pin back
- Craft glue or glue gun
- Heavy metallic cord (for amounts see Color Key).

CUTTING INSTRUCTIONS
For Light Bulb, cut three according to graph.

STITCHING INSTRUCTIONS:
1: Using colors and stitches indicated, work pieces according to graph; with matching colors, overcast edges of pieces.

NOTE: Cut one 28" [71.1cm] and one 6" [15.2cm] length of green cord.
2: For Necklace, glue ends of 28" length to wrong side of one Light Bulb; for Ornament, glue ends of 6" length to wrong side of one Light Bulb. For Pin, glue pin back to wrong side of remaining Light Bulb.

Light Bulb
(10w x 17h-hole pieces)
Cut 3. Work 1; substituting green & gold for red, work one in each color.

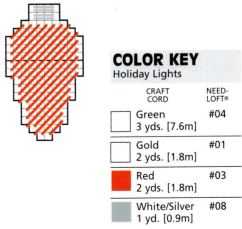

COLOR KEY
Holiday Lights

	CRAFT CORD	NEED-LOFT®
☐ Green 3 yds. [7.6m]		#04
☐ Gold 2 yds. [1.8m]		#01
▧ Red 2 yds. [1.8m]		#03
▨ White/Silver 1 yd. [0.9m]		#08

Snowman Pen Toppers

Designed by Carol Krob

Make writing fun with these quick-to-make pen toppers.

SIZE
Each is 2½" x 3" [6.4cm x 7.6cm], not
including pen.

MATERIALS
- ½ sheet of 10-mesh plastic canvas
- Two red 9mm round cabochons
- 18" [45.7cm] length of ⅛" [3mm] white
  satin ribbon
- One each red and green ¼" [6mm] pom-poms
- Decorative pen
- Craft glue or glue gun
- 5 yds. [4.6m] of gold ⅛" [3mm]
  metallic ribbon
- No. 3 pearl cotton (coton perlé) (for amounts
  see Color Key).

CUTTING INSTRUCTIONS
  A: For Front #1 and Back #1, cut one each
according to graphs.

  B: For Front #2 and Back #2, cut one each
according to graphs.

STITCHING INSTRUCTIONS
1: Using colors and stitches indicated, work
pieces according to graphs.

2: Using colors and emboridery stitches
indicated, embroider detail on Front A and
Front B pieces as indicated on graphs.

3: With metallic ribbon, whipstitch corresponding Front and Back pieces wrong sides together
as indicated; overcast unfinished edges.

NOTE: *Cut satin ribbon in half; tie each length
into a bow.*

4: Glue pom-poms, cabochons and bows to
each Front as indicated.

A – Front #1
(24w x 29h-hole piece)
Cut 1 & work.
Whipstitch to Back #1 between arrows.

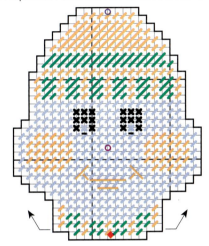

A – Back #1
(24w x 29h-hole piece)
Cut 1 & work.
Whipstitch to Front #1 between arrows.

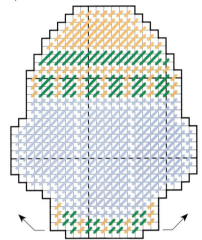

B – Front #2
(24w x 29h-hole piece)
Cut 1 & work.
Whipstitch to Back #2 between arrows.

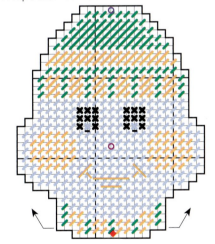

B – Back #2
(24w x 29h-hole piece)
Cut 1 & work.
Whipstitch to Front #2 between arrows.

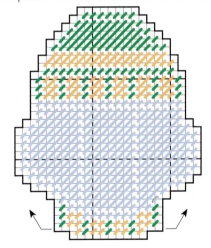

COLOR KEY
Snowman Pen Toppers

	NO. 3 PEARL COTTON	DMC®
White	8 yds. [7.3m]	White
Red	6 yds. [5.5m]	#321
Vy. Dk. Emerald Green	4 yds. [3.7m]	#909
Black	1 yd. [0.9m]	#310

STITCH KEY
⊟ Backstitch/Straight

PLACEMENT KEY
○ Pom-Pom
○ Cabochon
◆ Bow

Autumn Leaves Coasters

Designed by Debbie Tabor

Bring fall inside with this colorful Autumn coaster set.

SIZES
Each Coaster is 4½" x 4½" [11.4cm x 11.4cm]; Holder is 1⅞" x 5¼" x 2¼" tall [4.8cm x 13.3cm x 5.7cm].

MATERIALS
- One sheet of 7-mesh plastic canvas
- Six-strand embroidery floss (for amounts see Color Key)
- Worsted-weight or plastic canvas yarn (for amounts see Color Key).

CUTTING INSTRUCTIONS
   A: For Leaves #1-#4, cut one each according to graphs.
   B: For Acorn #1 and #2, cut one each according to graphs.
   C: For Holder Sides, cut two according to graph.
   D: For Holder Back and Bottom, cut two (one for Back and one for Bottom) 28w x 10h-holes (no graphs).

STITCHING INSTRUCTIONS:
1: Using colors and stitches indicated, work A-C pieces according to graphs; work D pieces using black and continental stitch. Omittng attachment edges, with matching colors as shown in photo, overcast edges of A and B pieces.

2: Using yarn and six strands floss in colors and embroidery stitches indicated, embroider detail on A and B pieces as indicated on graphs.

3: For Holder, whipstitch B-D pieces together according to Holder Assembly Diagram; with black, overcast remaining unfinished edges of Holder.

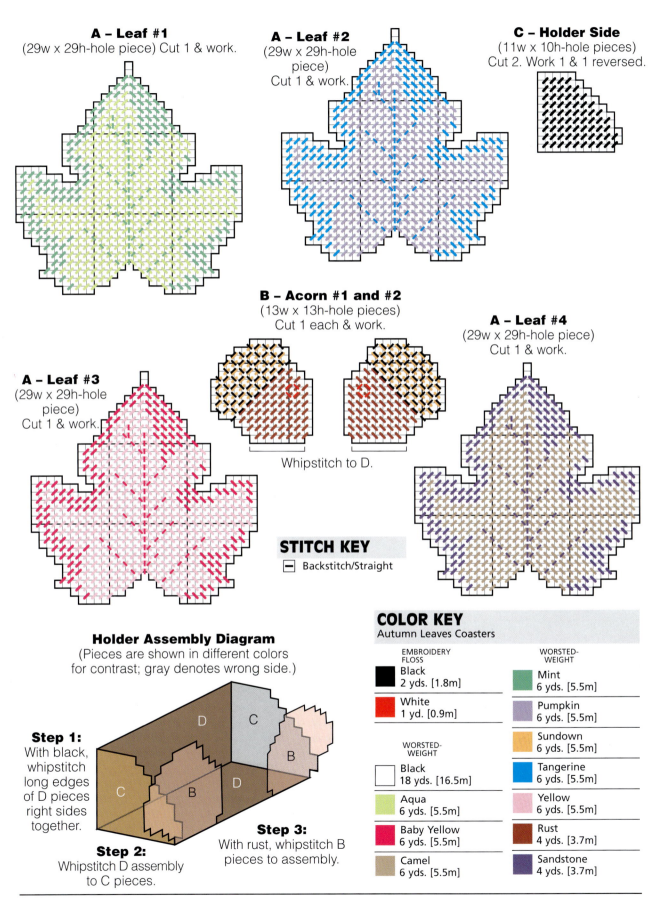

A – Leaf #1
(29w x 29h-hole piece) Cut 1 & work.

A – Leaf #2
(29w x 29h-hole piece)
Cut 1 & work.

C – Holder Side
(11w x 10h-hole pieces)
Cut 2. Work 1 & 1 reversed.

B – Acorn #1 and #2
(13w x 13h-hole pieces)
Cut 1 each & work.

Whipstitch to D.

A – Leaf #4
(29w x 29h-hole piece)
Cut 1 & work.

A – Leaf #3
(29w x 29h-hole piece)
Cut 1 & work.

STITCH KEY

⊟ Backstitch/Straight

Holder Assembly Diagram
(Pieces are shown in different colors
for contrast; gray denotes wrong side.)

Step 1:
With black, whipstitch long edges of D pieces right sides together.

Step 2:
Whipstitch D assembly to C pieces.

Step 3:
With rust, whipstitch B pieces to assembly.

COLOR KEY
Autumn Leaves Coasters

EMBROIDERY FLOSS	
■	Black 2 yds. [1.8m]
■	White 1 yd. [0.9m]

WORSTED-WEIGHT	
□	Black 18 yds. [16.5m]
■	Aqua 6 yds. [5.5m]
■	Baby Yellow 6 yds. [5.5m]
■	Camel 6 yds. [5.5m]

WORSTED-WEIGHT	
■	Mint 6 yds. [5.5m]
■	Pumpkin 6 yds. [5.5m]
■	Sundown 6 yds. [5.5m]
■	Tangerine 6 yds. [5.5m]
■	Yellow 6 yds. [5.5m]
■	Rust 4 yds. [3.7m]
■	Sandstone 4 yds. [3.7m]

Turkey Pilgrim

Designed by Marlene Hippen

Add a finishing touch of humor to your Thanksgiving dinner.

SIZE
Each is about 2¾" x 4¼" [7cm x 10.8cm].

MATERIALS
• ½ sheet of 7-mesh plastic canvas
• Worsted-weight or plastic canvas yarn
  (for amounts see Color Key).

CUTTING INSTRUCTIONS
For Napkin Rings, cut two according to graph.

STITCHING INSTRUCTIONS:
1: Using colors indicated and continental stitch, work pieces according to graph; with matching colors, overcast cutout and outer edges of pieces.
2: Using colors and embroidery stitches indicated, embroider detail on each piece as indicated on graph.

STITCH KEY
- ⊟ Backstitch/Straight
- ⊡ French Knot

Napkin Ring
(18w x 28h-hole pieces)
Cut 2 & work.

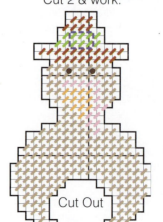

Cut Out

COLOR KEY
Turkey Pilgrim

	WORSTED-WEIGHT
Tan	15 yds. [13.7m]
Rust	4 yds. [3.7m]
Apple	1 yd. [0.9m]
Orange	1 yd. [0.9m]
Red	1 yd. [0.9m]
Brown	½ yd. [0.5m]
Gold	½ yd. [0.5m]

Wide-eyed Kitties

Designed by Kathy Wirth

Cat lovers will get a kick out of this clever clip and fridgie.

SIZES
Clip is ⅝" x 4" x 5¼" [1.6cm x 10.2cm x 13.3cm]; Fridgie is 2½" x 3½" [6.4cm x 8.9cm].

MATERIALS
- ¼ sheet each of 7-mesh and 10-mesh plastic canvas
- Two of each ⅝" [16mm] and ½" [13mm] yellow 2-holed buttons
- ¾" [19mm] mini spring wooden clothespin
- One ⅜" [10mm] and one ¼" [6mm] gold jingle bell
- Three 2" [5.1cm] magnetic strips
- Craft glue or glue gun
- Six-strand embroidery floss (for amounts see Color Key).
- Worsted-weight or plastic canvas yarn (for amounts see Color Key).

CUTTING INSTRUCTIONS
A: For Fronts, cut one from 7-mesh for Clip and one from 10-mesh for Fridgie according to graph.

B: For Backs, cut one from 7-mesh for Clip and one from 10-mesh for Fridgie according to graph.

STITCHING INSTRUCTIONS:
1: Using yarn in colors and stitches indicated, work 7-mesh A and B pieces according to graphs; using twelve strands floss in colors and stitches indicated, work 10-mesh A and B pieces according to graphs. With matching colors, overcast edges of pieces.

2: Using yarn and three strands floss in colors and embroidery stitches indicated, embroider detail on each piece as indicated on graphs.

3: For eyes, with black floss, sew ⅝" buttons to Clip Front and ½" buttons to Fridgie Front as shown in photo.

4: For Clip, using grenadine yarn, tack ⅜" bell to front as shown. Glue one side of clothespin to wrong side of A and opposite side of clothespin to right side of B. Glue two magnetic strips to wrong side of assembly.

5: For Fridgie, using cranberry floss, tack ¼" bell to front as shown. Glue A to right side of B (see photo); glue magnetic strip to wrong side of assembly.

A – Front
(21w x 24h-hole pieces)
Cut 1 from 7-mesh for Clip & 1
from 10-mesh for Fridgie.

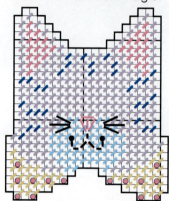

B – Back
(25w x 34h-hole pieces)
Cut 1 from 7-mesh for Clip & 1
from 10-mesh for Fridgie.

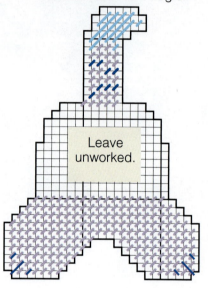

Leave unworked.

COLOR KEY
Wide-eyed Kitties

3-STRAND EMBROIDERY FLOSS	DMC®		WORSTED-WEIGHT	RED HEART CLASSIC®
■ Vy. Black 2 yds. [1.8m]	#310		Lavender 8 yds. [7.3m]	#584

6-STRAND EMBROIDERY FLOSS	DMC®			
Vy. Dk. Lavender 14 yds. [12.8m]	#208		Black 2 yds. [1.8m]	#12
Black 3 yds. [2.7m]	#310		Grenadine 2 yds. [1.8m]	#730
Cranberry 3 yds. [2.7m]	#603		White 2 yds. [1.8m]	#01
Lemon 3 yds. [2.7m]	#307		Yellow 2 yds. [1.8m]	#230
White 3 yds. [2.7m]	White			

STITCH KEY
⊟ Backstitch/Straight
⊡ French Knot

Night Night Moon

Designed by Michele Wilcox

This sleepytime moon motif will be perfect on a nursery doorstop.

SIZE
2¾" x 4½" x 7¾" tall [7cm x 11.4cm x 19.7cm], including Moon and Star.

MATERIALS
- Two sheets of 7-mesh plastic canvas
- One 5" [12.7cm] plastic canvas star shape
- A brick or zip-close bag filled with gravel or other weighting material
- Craft glue or glue gun
- No. 5 pearl cotton (coton perlé) or six-strand embroidery floss (for amount see Color Key).
- Worsted-weight or plastic canvas yarn (for amounts see Color Key).

CUTTING INSTRUCTIONS
A: For Cover Sides, cut two 26w x 51h-holes (no graph).

B: For Cover Ends, cut two 16w x 51h-holes (no graph).

C: For Cover Top and Bottom, cut two (one for Top and one for Bottom) 26w x 16h-holes (no graph).

D: For Moon, cut one according to graph.

E: For Star, cut one from star shape according to graph.

STITCHING INSTRUCTIONS:
1: Using colors and stitches indicated, work A-C pieces according to Cover Stitch Pattern Guide and D and E pieces according to graphs. With matching colors, overcast edges of D and E pieces.

2: Using pearl cotton or three strands floss and backstitch, embroider detail on D as indicated on graph.

3: For Cover, with dark royal, whipstitch A-C pieces wrong sides together, inserting weighting material before closing. Glue Moon and Star to one Cover Side as shown in photo.

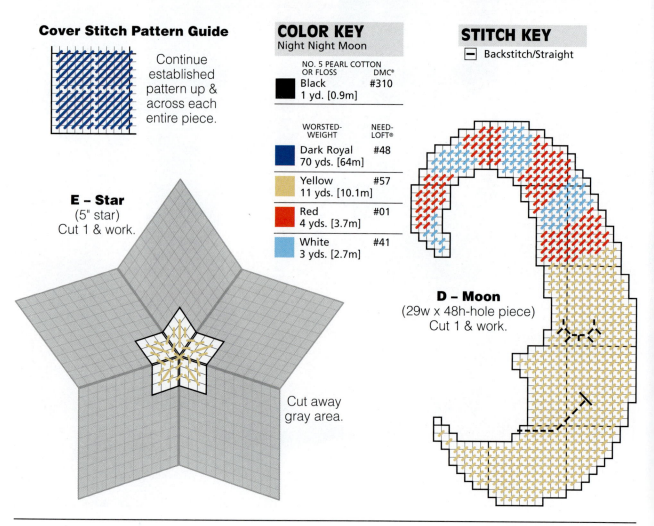

Cover Stitch Pattern Guide

Continue established pattern up & across each entire piece.

E – Star
(5" star)
Cut 1 & work.

Cut away gray area.

COLOR KEY
Night Night Moon

	NO. 5 PEARL COTTON OR FLOSS	DMC®
■	Black 1 yd. [0.9m]	#310

	WORSTED-WEIGHT	NEED-LOFT®
■	Dark Royal 70 yds. [64m]	#48
■	Yellow 11 yds. [10.1m]	#57
■	Red 4 yds. [3.7m]	#01
■	White 3 yds. [2.7m]	#41

STITCH KEY
- Backstitch/Straight

D – Moon
(29w x 48h-hole piece)
Cut 1 & work.

Playful Kitty

Designed by Marvin and Sandra Maxfield

*This playful kitty filled with goodies is sure
to delight a special friend.*

SIZE
3" x 6½" x 8¼" tall [7.6cm x 16.5cm x 21cm].

MATERIALS
• Two sheets of 7-mesh plastic canvas
• ½ yd. [0.5m] blue ½" [13mm] satin ribbon
• Craft glue or glue gun
• Worsted-weight or plastic canvas yarn (for amounts see Color Key).

CUTTING INSTRUCTIONS
   A: For Sides #1 and #2, cut one each according to graphs.
   B: For Ends, cut two 19w x 30h-holes.
   C: For Bottom, cut one 24w x 19h-holes (no graph).

STITCHING INSTRUCTIONS
NOTE: C is not worked.

1: Using colors and stitches indicated, work A and B pieces according to graphs; omitting attachment edges, with yellow, overcast cutout and outer edges of A pieces.

2: Using black and embroidery stitches indicated, embroider detail on A pieces as indicated on graphs.

3: With yellow, whipstitch and assemble pieces as indicated and according to Basket Assembly Diagram. Tie ribbon into a bow around tail of one Kitty as shown in photo.

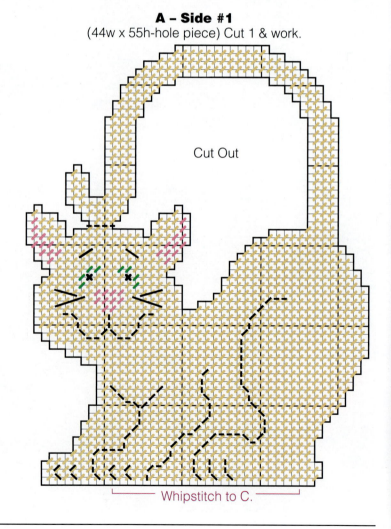

A – Side #1
(44w x 55h-hole piece) Cut 1 & work.

Cut Out

Whipstitch to C.

B – End
(19w x 30h-hole pieces)
Cut 2 & work.

Whipstitch to C.

A – Side #2
(44w x 554h-hole piece) Cut 1 & work.

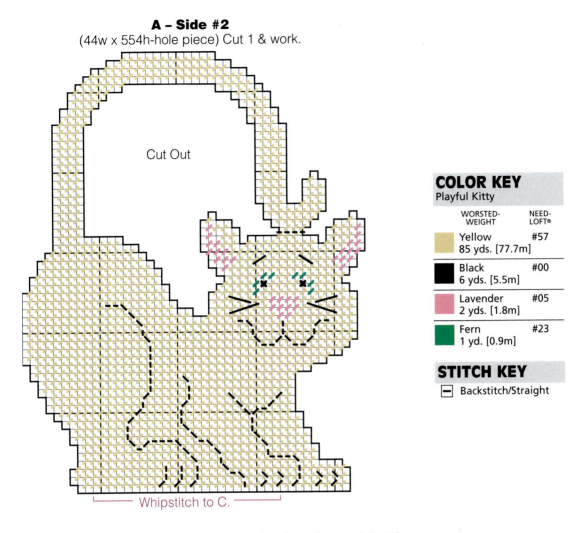

Cut Out

COLOR KEY
Playful Kitty

		WORSTED-WEIGHT	NEED-LOFT®
	Yellow	85 yds. [77.7m]	#57
	Black	6 yds. [5.5m]	#00
	Lavender	2 yds. [1.8m]	#05
	Fern	1 yd. [0.9m]	#23

STITCH KEY
⊟ Backstitch/Straight

Whipstitch to C.

Basket Assembly Diagram
(Pieces are shown in different colors for contrast; gray denotes wrong side.)

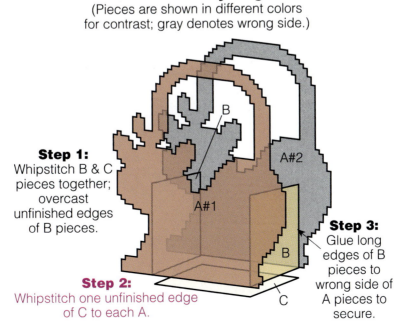

Step 1:
Whipstitch B & C pieces together; overcast unfinished edges of B pieces.

B

A#2

A#1

Step 3:
Glue long edges of B pieces to wrong side of A pieces to secure.

Step 2:
Whipstitch one unfinished edge of C to each A.

B

C

Kritter Keepers

Designed by Sandra Miller Maxfield

Keep crayons from rolling off the desktop with these clever kritter keepers.

SIZE
Each is about 1" x 1½" x 3½" [2.5cm x 3.8cm x 8.9cm], not including hands, paws, feet or tails.

MATERIALS
- ½ sheet of clear and scrap piece of 7-mesh plastic canvas
- Three pair of 7mm wiggle eyes in colors of choice
- Two black and four white 5mm pom-poms
- Craft glue or glue gun
- Worsted-weight or plastic canvas yarn (for amounts see Color Key).

CUTTING INSTRUCTIONS
NOTE: Use white for F pieces and clear canvas for remaining pieces.

A: For Gator, Kitty and Puppy Bodies, cut one each according to graphs.
B: For Arms, cut six (two for each Kritter) according to graph.
C: For Kitty and Puppy Paws, cut four (two for each Kritter) according to graph.
D: For Kitty Tail, cut one according to graph.
E: For Gator Mouth Top and Bottom, cut one each according to graphs.
F: For Gator Top and Bottom Teeth, cut one each according to graphs.
G: For Gator Feet, cut two according to graph.
H: For Gator Tail, cut one according to graph.
I: For Puppy Tail, cut two according to graph.

STITCHING INSTRUCTIONS:
NOTE: F pieces are not worked.

1: Using colors indicated and continental stitch, work A-E and G-I pieces according to graphs.

2: Using bright green and French knot, embroider detail on Top E as indicated on graph.

3: For each Body, with matching colors, fold and whipstitch one A wrong sides together as indicated; overcast unfinished edges.

4: For Gator mouth, with bright green, whipstitch Top E and Top F pieces together as indicated; overcast unfinished edges of E; repeat with Bottom E and Bottom F pieces. Holding Gator Mouth pieces wrong sides together, glue to Gator Body as shown.

5: For each Kritter, glue Arms, Feet, Paws and Tail to corresponding Body as indicated and as shown in photo. Glue one black and two white pom-poms together and to Puppy Body as shown; repeat with remaining pom-poms and Kitty Body. Glue two wiggle eyes to each Body as shown.

B – Arm
(4w x 9h-hole pieces)
Cut 6 from clear. Work 2; substituting bright yellow & bright blue for bright green, work 2 in each color.

C – Kitty & Puppy Paw
(5w x 6h-hole pieces)
Cut 4 from clear. Work 2 for Kitty; substituting bright blue for bright yellow, work 2 for Puppy.

D – Kitty Tail
(3w x 9h-hole piece)
Cut 1 from clear & work.

COLOR KEY
Kritter Keepers

	WORSTED-WEIGHT	NEED-LOFT®
Bright Green	12 yds. [11m]	#61
Bright Blue	10 yds. [9.1m]	#60
Bright Yellow	10 yds. [9.1m]	#63
Royal	2 yds. [1.8m]	#32

STITCH KEY
- ⊙ French Knot

A – Puppy Body
(12w x 50h-hole piece)
Cut 1 from clear & work.
Whipstitch between arrows.

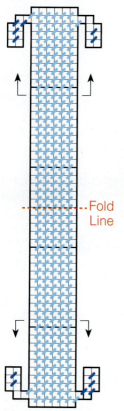

Fold Line

Whipstitch between arrows.

A – Gator Body
(7w x 50h-hole piece)
Cut 1 from clear & work.
Whipstitch between arrows.

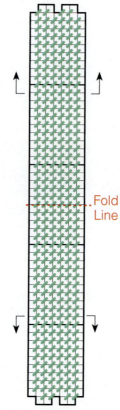

Fold Line

Whipstitch between arrows.

A – Kitty Body
(10w x 40h-hole piece)
Cut 1 from clear & work.
Whipstitch between arrows.

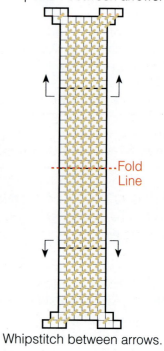

Fold Line

Whipstitch between arrows.

I – Puppy Tail
(8w x 6h-hole piece)
Cut 2 from clear & work through
both thicknesses as one.

H – Gator Tail
(7w x 13h-hole piece)
Cut 1 from clear & work.
Glue to Gator Body.

F – Gator Top Teeth
(17w x 1h-hole piece)
Cut 1 from white.

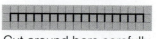

Cut around bars carefully.

F – Gator Bottom Teeth
(12w x 1h-hole piece)
Cut 1 from white.

Cut around bars carefully.

E – Gator Mouth Bottom
(4w x 6h-hole piece)
Cut 1 from clear & work.
Glue to Gator Body.

Whipstitch to Bottom
F between arrows.

E – Gator Mouth Top
(4w x 8h-hole piece)
Cut 1 from clear & work.
Glue to Gator Body.

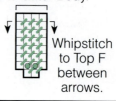

Whipstitch to Top F between arrows.

G – Gator Foot
(5w x 6h-hole pieces)
Cut 2 from clear & work

Tiger Windsock

Designed by Sandra Miller Maxfield

Decorate your patio or porch with this colorful windsock.

SIZE
Covers a 20 fl. oz. {592ml] plastic bottle.

MATERIALS
- One sheet of 7-mesh plastic canvas
- 3 yds. [2.7m] of ½" [13mm] orange satin ribbon
- 3½ yds. [3.2m] of ½" [13mm] blue satin ribbon
- One plastic bottle
- Country blue acrylic paint
- Craft glue or glue gun
- Worsted-weight or plastic canvas yarn (for amounts see Color Key).

CUTTING INSTRUCTIONS
A: For Side, cut one according to graph.
B: For Ears, cut two according to graph.
C: For Nose, cut one according to graph.
D: For Tail, cut one according to graph.

STITCHING INSTRUCTIONS
NOTE: With acrylic paint, paint bottle cap; let dry.

1: Using colors and stitches indicated, work A-D pieces according to graphs. With bright orange for Tail and with matching colors, overcast edges of B-D pieces.

2: Using black (Separate into individual plies, if desired.) and embroidery stitches indicated, embroider detail on A.

3: With bright orange, whipstitch short edges of A wrong sides together as indicated on graph; overcast unfinished edges (Do not overcast cutout edges.).

NOTES: Cut blue ribbon into seven 18" [45.7cm] lengths. Cut orange ribbon into six 18" [45.7cm] lengths.

4: Beginning at center front, thread one blue ribbon through cutouts on Side. Glue remaining ribbons to inside of Holder as shown in photo. Insert bottle into Holder: tie ribbon into a bow and trim ends as desired.

5: Glue Nose and Ears to Side as indicated and as shown and right side of Tail to bottom of back seam. Hang as desired.

A – Side
(68w x 51h-hole piece)
Cut 1 & work.

Cut out
gray areas.

Whipstitch

Whipstitch

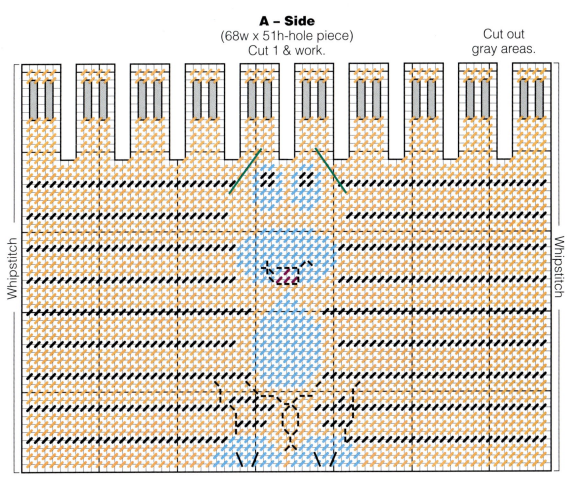

B – Ear
(8w x 4h-hole pieces)
Cut 2 & work.

Glue to Side.

C – Nose
(7w x 9h-hole piece)
Cut 1 & work.

D – Tail
(13w x 26h-hole piece)
Cut 1 & work.

Glue to Side.

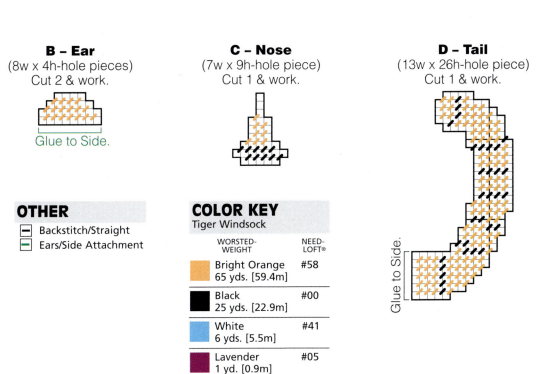

OTHER
⊟ Backstitch/Straight
⊟ Ears/Side Attachment

COLOR KEY
Tiger Windsock

	WORSTED-WEIGHT	NEED-LOFT®
■	Bright Orange 65 yds. [59.4m]	#58
■	Black 25 yds. [22.9m]	#00
■	White 6 yds. [5.5m]	#41
■	Lavender 1 yd. [0.9m]	#05

"Feed Me" Cat and Dog

Designed by Debbie Tabor

These feeding reminder magnets are as cute as they are helpful.

SIZES
Dog is 3¾" x 6¼" [9.5cm x 15.9cm];
Cat is 4" x 6¼" [10.2cm x 15.9cm].

MATERIALS
- One sheet of 7-mesh plastic canvas
- Two 2"-square [5.1cm] magnets
- Craft glue or glue gun
- Six-strand embroidery floss (for amounts see Color Key)
- Worsted-weight or plastic canvas yarn (for amounts see Color Key).

CUTTING INSTRUCTIONS:
A: For Dog, cut one according to graph.
B: For Bone Sides #1 and #2, cut one each according to graphs.
C: For Cat, cut one according to graph.
D: For Fish Side #1 and #2, cut one each according to graphs.

STITCHING INSTRUCTIONS
1: Using colors and stitches indicated, work pieces according to graphs.

2: Using six strands black floss, three strands white floss and embroidery stitches indicated, embroider detail on pieces as indicated on graphs.

3: For Bone, with white, whipstitch B pieces wrong sides together; secure Bone to Dog (see photo) leaving 1½" [3.8cm] space between center of Bone and bottom edge of Dog. For Fish, with bright orange, whipstitch D pieces wrong sides together; secure Fish to Cat (see photo) leaving 1½" [3.8cm] space between top edge of Fish and bottom edge of Cat.

4: Glue one magnet to wrong side of Dog and remaining magnet to wrong side of Cat.

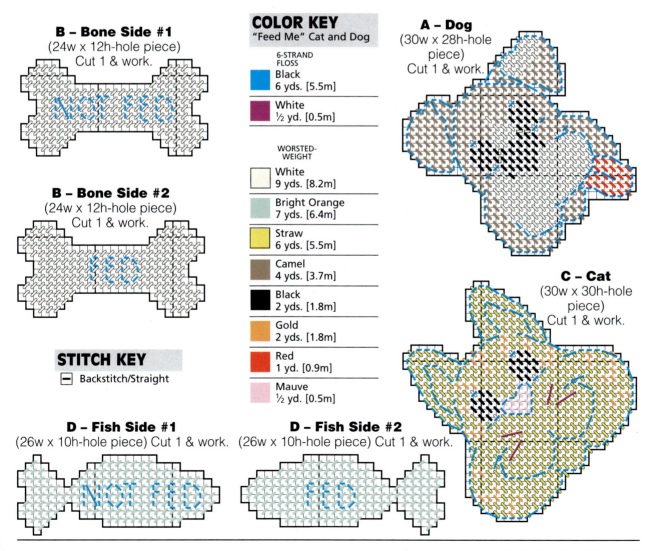

B – Bone Side #1
(24w x 12h-hole piece)
Cut 1 & work.

B – Bone Side #2
(24w x 12h-hole piece)
Cut 1 & work.

STITCH KEY
⊟ Backstitch/Straight

D – Fish Side #1
(26w x 10h-hole piece) Cut 1 & work.

D – Fish Side #2
(26w x 10h-hole piece) Cut 1 & work.

COLOR KEY
"Feed Me" Cat and Dog

6-STRAND FLOSS	
Black	6 yds. [5.5m]
White	½ yd. [0.5m]

WORSTED-WEIGHT	
White	9 yds. [8.2m]
Bright Orange	7 yds. [6.4m]
Straw	6 yds. [5.5m]
Camel	4 yds. [3.7m]
Black	2 yds. [1.8m]
Gold	2 yds. [1.8m]
Red	1 yd. [0.9m]
Mauve	½ yd. [0.5m]

A – Dog
(30w x 28h-hole piece)
Cut 1 & work.

C – Cat
(30w x 30h-hole piece)
Cut 1 & work.

Rosebud Eyeglass Case

Designed by Kimberly Suber

Keep your eyeglasses handy in this attractive rosebud case.

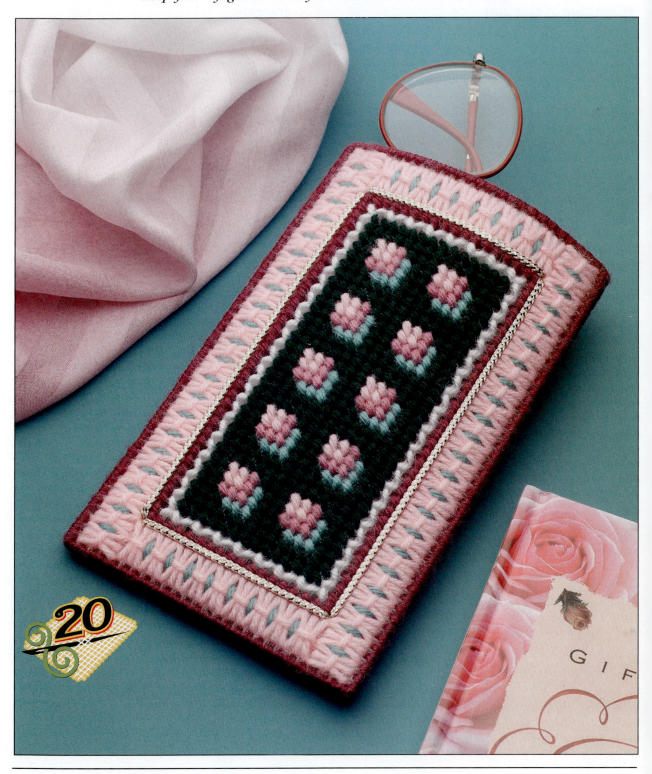

SIZE
4¼" x 7" [10.8cm x 17.8cm].

MATERIALS
• ½ sheet 7-mesh plastic canvas
• Heavy Metallic Cord (for amount see Color Key).
• Worsted-weight or plastic canvas yarn (for amounts see Color Key).

CUTTING INSTRUCTIONS
For Sides, cut two 27w x 45h-holes.

STITCHING INSTRUCTIONS
1: Using colors and stitches indicated, work Sides according to graph.

2: Using metallic cord and straight stitch, embroider detail on sides as indicated on graph.

3: With dk. rose, whipstitch Sides wrong sides together as indicated; overcast unfinished edges.

Side
(27w x 45h-hole pieces) Cut 2 & work.

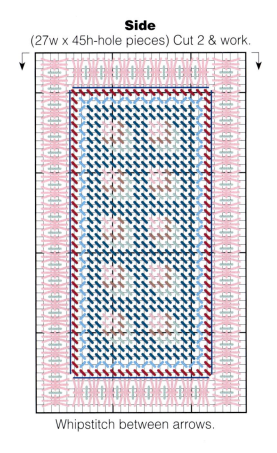

Whipstitch between arrows.

COLOR KEY
Rosebud Eyeglass Case

METALLIC CORD	NEED-LOFT®
White/Gold 2 yds. [1.8m]	#07

WORSTED-WEIGHT

Pink 16 yds. [14.6m]	
Dk. Green 9 yds. [8.2m]	
Dk. Rose 7 yds. [6.4m]	
Green 6 yds. [5.5m]	
White 3 yds. [2.7m]	
Rose 1 yd. [0.9m]	

STITCH KEY
⊟ Straight

Ladybug Flyswatter

Designed by Sandra Miller Maxfield

This pretty lady will be happy to keep flies at bay.

SIZE
4⅛" x about 18" long [10.5cm x 45.7cm], including wire handle.

MATERIALS
- ½ sheet each of black and red 7-mesh plastic canvas
- One large green-coated wire clothes hanger
- Wire cutters
- Worsted-weight or plastic canvas yarn (for amounts see Color Key).

CUTTING INSTRUCTIONS
A: For Body Front, cut one from red according to graph.

B: For Body Back, cut one from red according to graph.

C: For Wings, cut one from black according to graph.

D: For Spots, cut six from red according to graph.

E: For Eyes, cut two from black 2w x 2h-holes.

STITCHING INSTRUCTIONS
NOTE: A-D pieces are not worked

1: Using black and cross stitch, work E pieces according to graph. With Christmas red, whipstitch D pieces to C as indicated on graph.

2: Whipstitch wire hanger and A-E pieces together according to Flyswatter Assembly Diagram.

A – Body Front
(23w x 40h-hole piece)
Cut 1 from red & leave unworked.

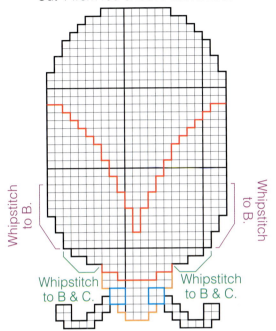

Whipstitch to B.

Whipstitch to B.

Whipstitch to B & C.

Whipstitch to B & C.

B – Body Back
(23w x 17h-hole piece)
Cut 1 from red & leave unworked.

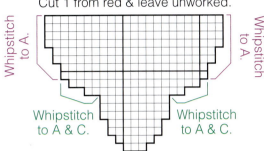

Whipstitch to A.

Whipstitch to A.

Whipstitch to A & C.

Whipstitch to A & C.

C – Wings
(27w x 23h-hole piece)
Cut 1 from black & leave unworked. Position D pieces over C & with Christmas red, whipstitch together.

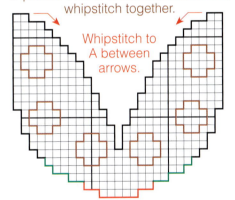

Whipstitch to A between arrows.

D – Spot
(4w x 4h-hole pieces)
Cut 6 from red & leave unworked.

E – Eye
(2w x 2h-hole pieces)
Cut 2 from black.
Position over A & work through both thicknesses.

Flyswatter Assembly Diagram
(Pieces are shown in different colors for contrast; spots & eyes not shown for clarity.)

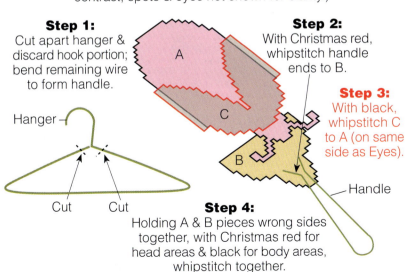

Step 1:
Cut apart hanger & discard hook portion; bend remaining wire to form handle.

Hanger

Cut   Cut

Step 2:
With Christmas red, whipstitch handle ends to B.

Step 3:
With black, whipstitch C to A (on same side as Eyes).

Handle

Step 4:
Holding A & B pieces wrong sides together, with Christmas red for head areas & black for body areas, whipstitch together.

COLOR KEY
Ladybug Flyswatter

	WORSTED-WEIGHT	NEED-LOFT®
■	Black 2 yds. [1.8m]	#00
□	Christmas Red 2 yds. [1.8m]	#02

ATTACHMENT KEY
- Eye
- Spot
- Wings/Body
- Body Front & Back

For Your Good Health

Designed by Kristine Loffredo

Show your appreciation to a special care-giver with this clever candy box.

SIZE
5" x 6½" x 7½" tall [12.7cm x 16.5cm x 19.1cm].

MATERIALS
- Two sheets of 7-mesh plastic canvas
- Two 12mm round wiggle eyes
- Craft glue or glue gun
- #16 medium metallic braid (for amount see Color Key);
- Worsted-weight or plastic canvas yarn (for amounts see Color Key).

CUTTING INSTRUCTIONS:
A: For Front, cut one 43w x 15h-holes.

B: For Back, cut one according to graph.

C: For Sides #1 and Sides #2, cut two (one for Side #1 and one for Side #2) 32w x 15h-holes.

D: For Bottom, cut one 43w x 32h-holes (no graph).

E: For Hands, cut two according to graph.

STITCHING INSTRUCTIONS
NOTE: D is not worked.

1: Using colors and stitches indicated, work A-C and E pieces according to graphs; with pink, overcast edges of E pieces.

2: Using braid and yarn (Separate yarn into individual plies, if desired.) in colors and embroidery stitches indicated, embroider detail on B as indicated on graph.

3: With matching colors, whipstitch A-D pieces together as indicated on graphs and according to Nurse Treat Box Assembly Illustration; overcast unfinished edges.

4: Glue Hands to Front as shown in photo. Glue wiggle eyes to Back as indicated.

COLOR KEY
For Your Good Health

METALLIC BRAID
- Sapphire — 2 yds. [1.8m]

WORSTED-WEIGHT
- White — 38 yds. [34.7m]
- Pink — 30 yds. [27.4m]
- Royal — 30 yds. [27.4m]
- Cinnamon — 10 yds. [9.1m]
- Red — 2 yds. [1.8m]

STITCH KEY
- Backstitch/Straight

ATTACHMENT KEY
- Wiggle Eye

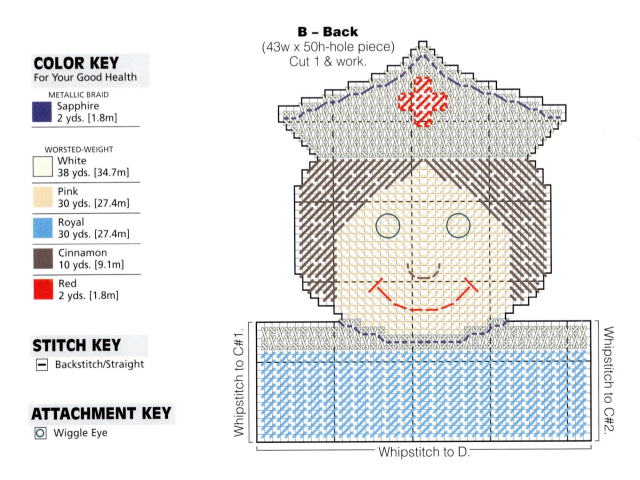

B – Back
(43w x 50h-hole piece)
Cut 1 & work.

Whipstitch to C#1.

Whipstitch to C#2.

Whipstitch to D.

COLOR KEY
For Your Good Health

METALLIC BRAID
Sapphire
2 yds. [1.8m]

WORSTED-WEIGHT
White
38 yds. [34.7m]

Pink
30 yds. [27.4m]

Royal
30 yds. [27.4m]

Cinnamon
10 yds. [9.1m]

Red
2 yds. [1.8m]

For Your Good Health Assembly Illustration
(Pieces are shown in different colors for contrast; gray denotes wrong side.)

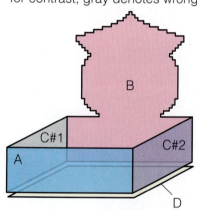

E – Hand
(16w x 12h-hole pieces)
Cut 2. Work 1 & 1 reversed.

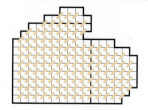

A – Front
(43w x 15h-hole piece)
Cut 1 & work.

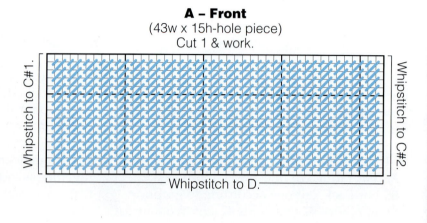

C – Side #1
(32w x 15h-hole piece)
Cut 1 & work.

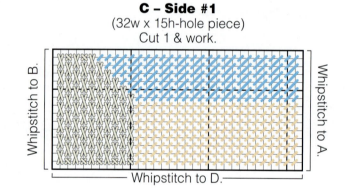

C – Side #2
(32w x 15h-hole piece)
Cut 1 & work.

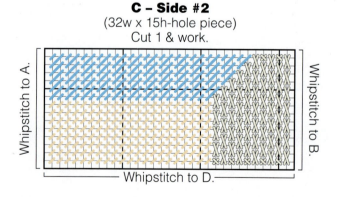

Graduation Day

Designed by Mary T. Cosgrove

Proudly display mementos of milestone moments.

SIZES

Diploma Frame is 5" x 4" tall [12.7cm x 10.2cm]; Diploma is 2" x 4¾" [5.1cm x 12.1cm]; Mortorboard Frame is 6" x 3½" tall [15.2cm x 8.9cm]; Mortorboard is 3¾" x 4¼" [9.5cm x 10.8cm].

MATERIALS

- One sheet of 7-mesh plastic canvas
- Heavy metallic craft cord (for amount see Color Key)
- Worsted-weight or plastic canvas yarn (for amounts see Color Key).

CUTTING INSTRUCTIONS

A: For Diploma Frame Front and Back, cut two (one for Front and one for Back) according to graph.

B: For Diploma Frame Stand, cut one 11w x 18h-holes (no graph).

C: For Diploma, cut one according to graph.

D: For Mortarboard Frame Front and Back, cut two (one for Front and one for Back) according to graph.

E: For Mortarboard Stand, cut one 22w x 11h-holes (no graph).

F: For Mortarboard, cut one according to graph.

STITCHING INSTRUCTIONS

NOTE: Back A, B, Back D and E pieces are not worked.

1: Using colors and stitches indicated, work Front A, C, Front D and F pieces according to graphs; with white for Mortarboard and with indicated and matching colors, overcast outer edges of C and F and cutout edges of Front A and Front D pieces.

2: Using gold cord and embroidery stitches indicated, embroider detail on Front A and C pieces as indicated on graphs.

3: With matching colors, whipstitch A and B pieces together according to Diploma Frame Assembly Diagram; whipstitch D and E pieces together according to Mortarboard Frame Assembly Diagram. Overcast unfinished edges.

A – Diploma Frame Front & Back
(33w x 29h-hole pieces) Cut 2. Work 1 for Front & leave 1 unworked for Back.

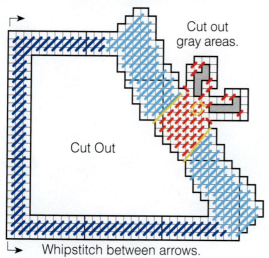

Cut out gray areas.

Cut Out

Whipstitch between arrows.

C – Diploma
(21w x 29h-hole piece) Cut 1 & work.

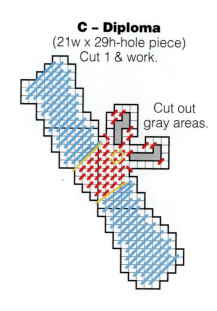

Cut out gray areas.

D – Mortarboard Frame Front & Back
(40w x 22h-hole pieces) Cut 2. Work 1 for Front & leave 1 unworked for Back.

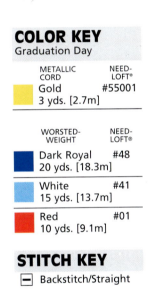

Overcast with white between arrows.

Cut Out

Whipstitch between arrows.

F – Mortarboard
(23w x 22h-hole piece) Cut 1 & work.

COLOR KEY
Graduation Day

METALLIC CORD		NEED-LOFT®
▨	Gold 3 yds. [2.7m]	#55001

WORSTED-WEIGHT		NEED-LOFT®
▨	Dark Royal 20 yds. [18.3m]	#48
▨	White 15 yds. [13.7m]	#41
▨	Red 10 yds. [9.1m]	#01

STITCH KEY
− Backstitch/Straight

Diploma Frame Assembly Diagram
(Pieces are shown in different colors for contrast.)
(back view)

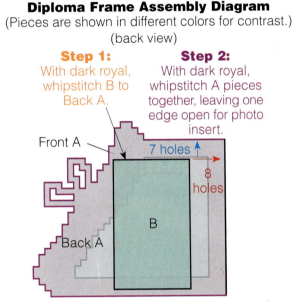

Step 1: With dark royal, whipstitch B to Back A.

Step 2: With dark royal, whipstitch A pieces together, leaving one edge open for photo insert.

Front A

Back A

7 holes

8 holes

B

Mortarboard Frame Assembly Diagram
(Pieces are shown in different colors for contrast; gray denotes wrong side.)

(back view)

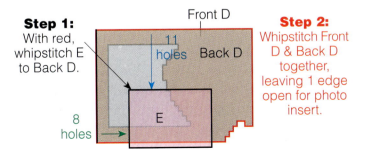

Step 1: With red, whipstitch E to Back D.

Front D

Back D

11 holes

8 holes

E

Step 2: Whipstitch Front D & Back D together, leaving 1 edge open for photo insert.

Apple Kitchen Set

Designed by Kristine Loffredo

The cook on your gift list will love these fresh and pretty accessories.

SIZES

Note Holder is 2" x 2½" x 3" tall [5.1cm x 6.4cm x 7.6cm]; Jar Lid Insert is 2½" across [6.4cm]; Book Cover fits a 2½" x 5" x 6½" [6.4cm x 12.7cm x 16.5cm] book or photo album.

MATERIALS

• Two sheets of 7-mesh plastic canvas 2½" x 5" x 6½" [6.4cm x 12.7cm x 16.5cm] book or photo album
• One small mouth jar ring
• Craft glue or glue gun
• Heavy metallic craft cord (for amount see Color Key).
• Worsted-weight or plastic canvas yarn (for amounts see Color Key).

CUTTING INSTRUCTIONS

A: For Note Holder Sides, cut two 16w x 21h-holes.

B: For Note Holder Bottom, cut one 16w x 12h-holes.

C: For Jar Lid Insert, cut one according to graph.

D: For Book Cover Front, cut one 46w x 35h-holes.

E: For Book Cover Spine, cut one 46w x 16h-holes.

F: For Book Cover Back, cut one 46w x 35h-holes.

G: For Book Cover Front Inside Flap, cut one 46w x 16h-holes.

H: For Book Cover Back Inside Flap, cut one 46w x 16h-holes.

I: For Large Flower, cut one according to graph.

J: For Small Flower, cut one according to graph.

K: For Leaves, cut two according to graph.

STITCHING INSTRUCTIONS

1: Using colors and stitches indicated, work pieces according to graphs; with matching colors, overcast edges of I-K pieces.

2: Using lavender and embroidery stitches indicated, embroider detail on I and J pieces as indicated on graphs.

3: For Note Holder, with holly, whipstitch A and B pieces wrong sides together as indicated; overcast unfinished edges.

4: For Jar Lid Insert, place inside a small mouth jar ring.

5: For Book Cover, with holly, whipstitch D-H pieces wrong sides together as indicated; overcast unfinished edges. Glue I-K pieces to Front as shown in photo.

I – Large Flower
(11w x 11h-hole piece)
Cut 1 & work.

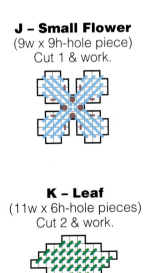

J – Small Flower
(9w x 9h-hole piece)
Cut 1 & work.

K – Leaf
(11w x 6h-hole pieces)
Cut 2 & work.

STITCH KEY

⊟ Backstitch/Straight
⊡ French Knot

COLOR KEY
Apple Kitchen Set

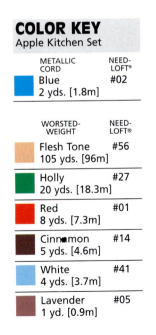

METALLIC CORD		NEED-LOFT®
■	Blue 2 yds. [1.8m]	#02

WORSTED-WEIGHT		NEED-LOFT®
■	Flesh Tone 105 yds. [96m]	#56
■	Holly 20 yds. [18.3m]	#27
■	Red 8 yds. [7.3m]	#01
■	Cinnamon 5 yds. [4.6m]	#14
■	White 4 yds. [3.7m]	#41
■	Lavender 1 yd. [0.9m]	#05

A – Note Holder Side
(16w x 21h-hole pieces)
Cut 2 & work.

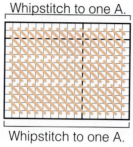

B – Note Holder Bottom
(16w x 12h-hole piece)
Cut 1 & work.

Whipstitch to one A.

Whipstitch to one A.

C – Jar Lid Insert
(16w x 17h-hole piece)
Cut 1 & work.

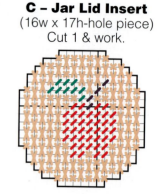

Whipstitch to B.

D – Book Cover Front
(46w x 35h-hole piece) Cut 1 & work.

Whipstitch to one long edge of E.

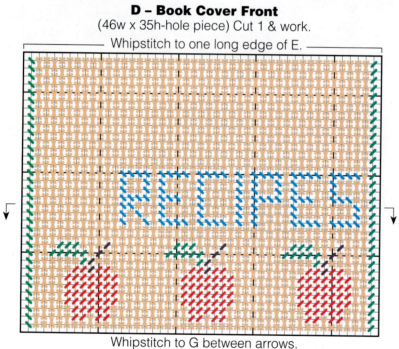
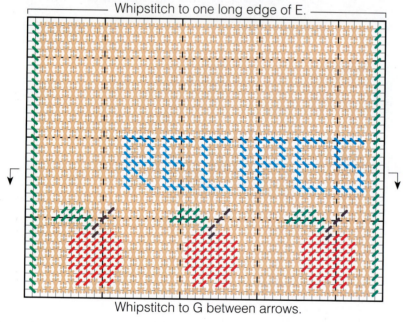

Whipstitch to G between arrows.

G – Book Cover Front Inside Flap
(46w x 16h-hole piece) Cut 1 & work.

Whipstitch to D between arrows.

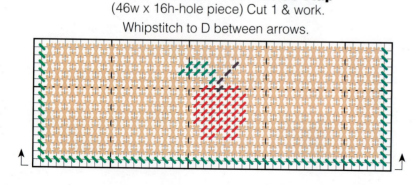

STITCH KEY

−	Backstitch/Straight
⊙	French Knot

COLOR KEY
Apple Kitchen Set

METALLIC CORD		NEED-LOFT®
■	Blue 2 yds. [1.8m]	#02

WORSTED-WEIGHT		NEED-LOFT®
■	Flesh Tone 105 yds. [96m]	#56
■	Holly 20 yds. [18.3m]	#27
■	Red 8 yds. [7.3m]	#01
■	Cinnamon 5 yds. [4.6m]	#14
■	White 4 yds. [3.7m]	#41
■	Lavender 1 yd. [0.9m]	#05

H – Book Cover Back Inside Flap
(46w x 16h-hole piece) Cut 1 & work.

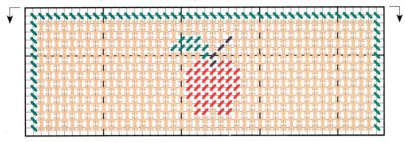

Whipstitch to F between arrows.

E – Book Cover Spine
(46w x 16h-hole piece) Cut 1 & work.
Whipstitch to F.

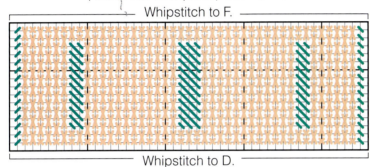

Whipstitch to D.

F – Book Cover Back
(46w x 35h-hole piece) Cut 1 & work.
Whipstitch to one long edge of E.

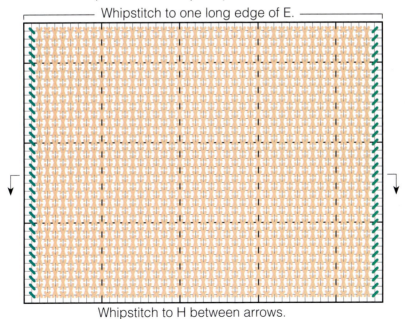

Whipstitch to H between arrows.

Family Favorites

Designed by Michele Wilcox

Filled with favorite recipes, this is the perfect gift for a new bride and groom.

SIZE
3½" x 5¾" x 6¾" tall [8.9cm x 14.6cm x 17.1cm].

MATERIALS
- One sheet of 7-mesh plastic canvas
- No. 3 pearl cotton (coton perlé) or six-strand embroidery floss (for amount see Color Key).
- Worsted-weight or plastic canvas yarn (for amounts see Color Key).

CUTTING INSTRUCTIONS
   A: For Front, cut one 37w x 23h-holes.
   B: For Back, cut one according to graph.
   C: For Sides, cut two 22w x 23h-holes.
   D: For Bottom, cut one 37w x 22h-holes (no graph).

STITCHING INSTRUCTIONS
NOTE: D is not worked.

1: Using colors and stitches indicated, work A-C according to graphs.

2: Using pearl cotton or six strands black floss and embroidery stitches indicated, embroider detail on A and B pieces as indicated on graphs.

3: With mermaid, whipstitch pieces together according to Box Assembly Illustration; with matching colors, overcast unfinished edges.

A – Front
(37w x 23h-hole piece) Cut 1 & work.

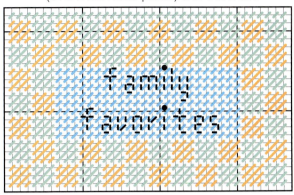

Box Assembly Illustration
(Pieces are shown in different colors for contrast; gray denotes wrong side.)

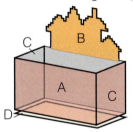

C – Side
(22w x 23h-hole pieces)
Cut 2 & work.

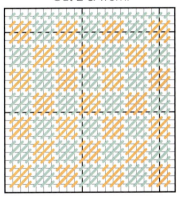

B – Back
(37w x 44h-hole piece) Cut 1 & work.

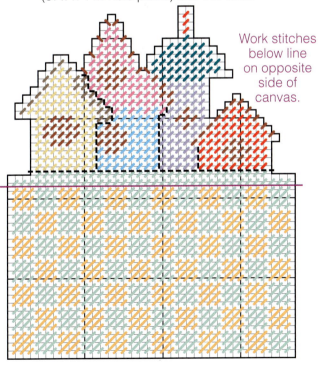

Work stitches below line on opposite side of canvas.

STITCH KEY

−	Backstitch/Straight
•	French Knot

COLOR KEY
Family Favorites

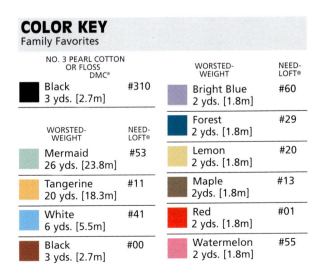

NO. 3 PEARL COTTON OR FLOSS DMC®			WORSTED-WEIGHT		NEED-LOFT®
■	Black 3 yds. [2.7m]	#310		Bright Blue 2 yds. [1.8m]	#60
				Forest 2 yds. [1.8m]	#29
WORSTED-WEIGHT		**NEED-LOFT®**		Lemon 2 yds. [1.8m]	#20
	Mermaid 26 yds. [23.8m]	#53		Maple 2yds. [1.8m]	#13
	Tangerine 20 yds. [18.3m]	#11		Red 2 yds. [1.8m]	#01
	White 6 yds. [5.5m]	#41		Watermelon 2 yds. [1.8m]	#55
	Black 3 yds. [2.7m]	#00			

Christmas Recipes

Designed by Michele Wilcox

Store your holiday favorites in this special box.

SIZE
3½" x 5¾" x 6½" tall [8.9cm x 14.6cm x 16.5cm].

MATERIALS
- One sheet of 7-mesh plastic canvas
- No. 5 pearl cotton (coton perlé) or six-strand embroidery floss (for amounts see Color Key).
- Worsted-weight or plastic canvas yarn (for amounts see Color Key).

CUTTING INSTRUCTIONS
A: For Back, cut one according to graph.
B: For Front, cut one 37w x 23h-holes.
C: For Sides, cut two 22w x 23h-holes.
D: For Bottom, cut one 37w x 22h-holes (no graph).

STITCHING INSTRUCTIONS
NOTE: D is not worked.

1: Using colors and stitches indicated, work A- C pieces according to graphs.

2: Using pearl cotton or floss in colors and embroidery stitches indicated, embroider detail on B piece as indicated on graph.

3: With red, whipstitch pieces together, forming box; with matching colors, overcast unfinished edges.

B – Front
(37w x 23h-hole piece) Cut 1 & work.

C – Side
(22w x 23h-hole pieces)
Cut 2 & work.

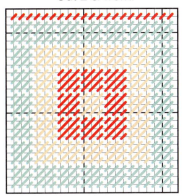

A – Back
(37w x 42h-hole piece)
Cut 1 & work.

Work stitches below line on opposite side of canvas.

Whipstitch to one C between arrows.

Whipstitch to one C between arrows.

COLOR KEY
Christmas Recipes

	NO. 5 PEARL COTTON OR FLOSS	DMC®
■	Black 2 yds. [1.8m]	#310
■	Bright Red 1 yd. [0.9m]	#666
■	Green 1 yd. [0.9m]	#699

	WORSTED-WEIGHT	NEED-LOFT®
■	Eggshell 27 yds. [24.7m]	#39
■	Holly 20 yds. [18.3m]	#27
■	Red 15 yds. [13.7m]	#01

STITCH KEY
⊟	Backstitch/Straight
⊡	French Knot

Mosaic Mugs

Designed by Mary T. Cosgrove

Serve a generous helping of holiday cheer in these pretty mugs.

SIZE
Each fits inside a 4" [10.2cm] tall plastic snap-together mug.

MATERIALS FOR ONE
- ½ sheet of 7-mesh plastic canvas
- Snap-together acrylic mug with white rim
- Worsted-weight or plastic canvas yarn (for amounts see individual Color Keys).

CUTTING INSTRUCTIONS
A: For Panel #1, cut one 65w x 23h-holes.
B: For Panel #2, cut one 65w x 23h-holes.
C: For Panel #3, cut one 65w x 23h-holes.
D: For Panel #4, cut one 65w x 23h-holes.

STITCHING INSTRUCTIONS
1: Using colors and stitches indicated, work Panel of choice according to graph.

2: With matching colors, whipstitch short edges together as indicated on graph; overcast unfinished edges.

3: Place Panel inside mug according to manufacturer's instructions.

A – Panel #1
(65w x 23h-hole piece) Cut 1 & work.

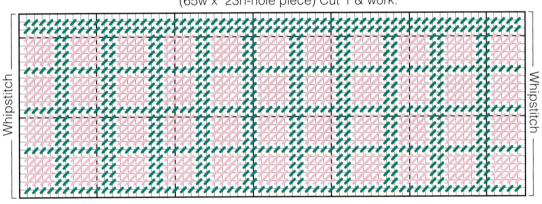

COLOR KEY
Panel #1

	WORSTED-WEIGHT	NEED-LOFT®
■ (green)	Christmas Green 13 yds. [11.9m]	#28
■ (pink)	White 11 yds. [10.1m]	#41

COLOR KEY
Panel #2

	WORSTED-WEIGHT	NEED-LOFT®
■ (red)	Christmas red 18 yds. [16.5m]	#02
■ (pink)	White 7 yds. [6.4m]	#41

B – Panel #2
(65w x 23h-hole piece) Cut 1 & work.

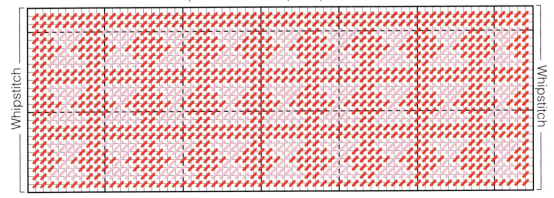

COLOR KEY
Panel #3

WORSTED-WEIGHT		NEED-LOFT®
	Bright Purple 17 yds. [15.6m]	#64
	White 8 yds. [7.3m]	#41

C – Panel #3
(65w x 23h-hole piece) Cut 1 & work.

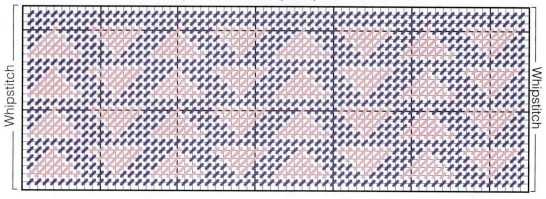

COLOR KEY
Panel #4

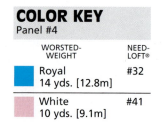

WORSTED-WEIGHT		NEED-LOFT®
	Royal 14 yds. [12.8m]	#32
	White 10 yds. [9.1m]	#41

D – Panel #4
(65w x 32h-hole piece) Cut 1 & work.

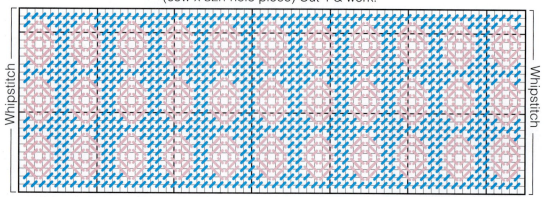

Sweetheart Frame

Designed by Kristine Loffredo

Keep a loved one's photo nearby in this lovable frame.

SIZE

2" x 5¼" x 6¼" tall [5.1cm x 13.3cm x 15.9cm].

MATERIALS

- One sheet of 7-mesh plastic canvas
- Four ½" [13mm] white ribbon roses
- Craft glue or glue gun
- Heavy metallic craft cord (for amounts see Color Key).
- Worsted-weight or plastic canvas yarn (for amount see Color Key).

CUTTING INSTRUCTIONS

A: For Frame Top Piece, cut one according to graph.

B: For Frame Front & Backing, cut two (one for Front and one for Backing) 34w x 42h-holes.

C: For Stand Long Piece, cut one 12w x 27h-holes (no graph).

D: For Stand Short Piece, cut one 12w x 12h-holes (no graph).

PLACEMENT KEY

☐ Frame Top/Frame Front

B – Frame Front & Backing
(34w x 42h-hole pieces)
Cut 2. Work 1 & leave 1 unworked for Backing.

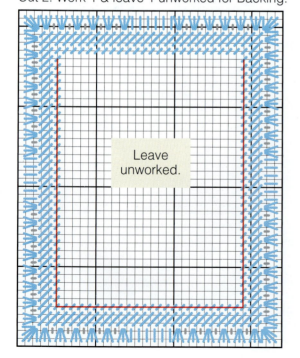

Leave unworked.

STITCHING INSTRUCTIONS

NOTE: Backing B, C and D pieces are not worked.

1: Using colors and stitches indicated, work A and Front B pieces according to graphs; with white/silver cord, overcast cutout and outer edges of A.

2: Whipstitch and assemble ribbon roses and A-D pieces according to Frame Assembly Diagram.

A – Frame Top Piece
(24w x 32h-hole piece) Cut 1 & work.

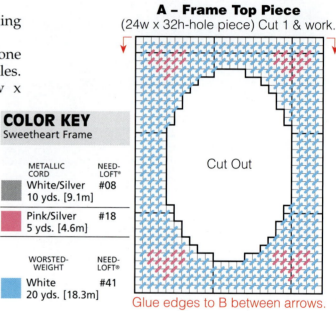

Cut Out

Glue edges to B between arrows.

COLOR KEY
Sweetheart Frame

METALLIC CORD	NEED-LOFT®
White/Silver 10 yds. [9.1m]	#08
Pink/Silver 5 yds. [4.6m]	#18

WORSTED-WEIGHT	NEED-LOFT®
White 20 yds. [18.3m]	#41

Frame Assembly Diagram
(Pieces are shown in different colors for contrast; gray denotes wrong side.)

(back view)

Step 1:
With white, whipstitch C to Backing B.

Step 2:
Whipstitch C & D pieces together; whipstitch D to Backing B.

Step 3:
With silver/pink, whipstitch Front B & Backing B wrong sides together.

Step 5:
Glue one ribbon rose to each corner of A.

Step 4:
Center A & glue to right side of Front B around Side & Bottom edges, leaving top edge open for photo insert.

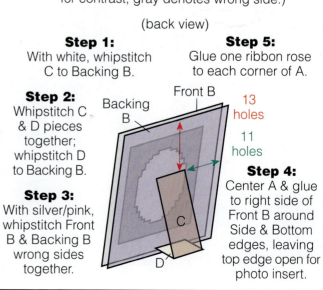

13 holes

11 holes

Butterfly Coasters

Designed by Mike Vickery

Nature lovers will appreciate these colorful beauties.

SIZES

Each Coaster is 4¾" x 5" [12.1cm x 12.7cm];
Holder is 4¾" square x 5" tall [12.1cm x
12.7cm] including Handle.

MATERIALS

- Two sheets of 7-mesh plastic canvas
- Craft glue or glue gun
- Worsted-weight or plastic canvas yarn
  (for amounts see Color Key).

CUTTING INSTRUCTIONS

A: For Butterflies #1-#4, cut one each
according to graphs.

B: For Holder Sides, cut four 31w x
10h-holes.

C: For Holder Handle, cut one 3w x
69h-holes.

D: For Holder Bottom, cut four 31w x 31h-
holes (no graph).

STITCHING INSTRUCTIONS

NOTE: D is not worked.

1: Using colors and stitches indicated, work
A-C pieces according to graphs; with matching
colors as shown in photo, overcast edges of A
and C pieces.

2: Using black (Separate into individual plies,
if desired.) and French knot, embroider detail
on A pieces as indicated on graphs.

3: With matching colors, whipstitch
and assemble B-D pieces according to
Holder Assembly Illustration; overcast
unfinished edges.

A – Butterfly #1
(32w x 30h-hole piece)
Cut 1 & work.

STITCH KEY

⊙ French Knot

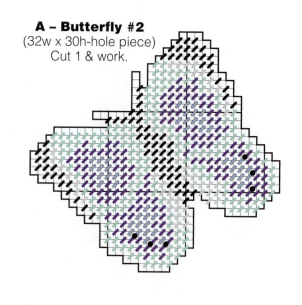

A – Butterfly #2
(32w x 30h-hole piece)
Cut 1 & work.

COLOR KEY
Butterfly Coasters

WORSTED-WEIGHT		WORSTED-WEIGHT	
■	Grenadine 28 yds. [25.6m]	■	Lavender 3 yds. [2.7m]
■	Amethyst 12 yds. [11m]	■	Light Periwinkle 3 yds. [2.7m]
■	Black 12 yds. [11m]	■	Yellow 3 yds. [2.7m]
■	Country Red 5 yds. [4.6m]	■	Light Lavender 1 yd. [0.9m]
■	Medium Coral 5 yds. [4.6m]	■	Maize 1 yd. [0.9m]
■	Nickel 5 yds. [4.6m]	■	Pink 1 yd. [0.9m]
■	True Blue 5 yds. [4.6m]	■	Sky 1 yd. [0.9m]

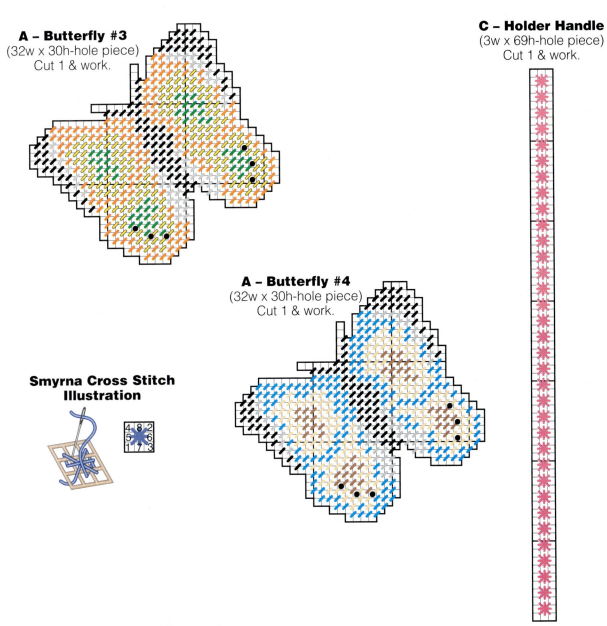

A – Butterfly #3
(32w x 30h-hole piece)
Cut 1 & work.

C – Holder Handle
(3w x 69h-hole piece)
Cut 1 & work.

A – Butterfly #4
(32w x 30h-hole piece)
Cut 1 & work.

Smyrna Cross Stitch Illustration

4	8	2
5		6
1	7	3

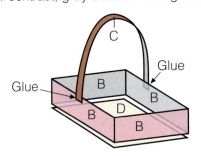

Holder Assembly Illustration
(Pieces are shown in different colors
for contrast; gray denotes wrong side.)

Glue

Glue

B – Holder Side
(31w x 10h-hole pieces) Cut 4 & work.

Snowflake Napkin Cuffs

Designed by Joan Green

These delightful accessories are elegant enough for a formal holiday table.

SIZE
Each is about 3½" x 6" [8.9cm x 15.2cm].

MATERIALS
- One sheet of 7-mesh plastic canvas
- 72 white 2.5mm pearl beads
- Beading needle and white sewing thread
- Metallic plastic canvas yarn (for amount see Color Key).
- Worsted-weight or plastic canvas yarn (for amouns see Color Key).

CUTTING INSTRUCTIONS
For Napkin Holder Fronts & Backs, cut eight (four for Fronts and four for Backs) according to graph.

STITCHING INSTRUCTIONS
NOTE: Backs are not worked.

1: Using colors and stitches indicated, work one Front according to graph, substituting Motif #2-#4 for Motif #1, work remaining Fronts according to graph.

2: Using white arctic rays, embroider one Motif on each Front as indicated on Motifs #1-#4. With beading needle and thread, sew pearls to each Front as indicated.

3: Holding one Back to wrong side of each Front, with teal, whipstitch together as indicated.

OTHER
- Backstitch/Straight
- O Bead

Napkin Holder Front & Back
Motif #1
(22w x 40h-hole pieces)
Cut 8. Work 1 for Front, filling in uncoded areas using teal & continental stitch. Substituting Motifs #2-#4 for Motif #1, work one each for Fronts; leave 4 unworked for Backs.

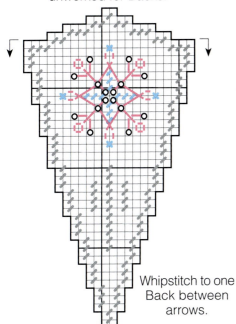

Whipstitch to one Back between arrows.

Motif #4
Substitute Motif #4 for Motif #1 on A graph for 1 Front.

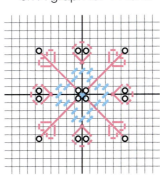

Motif #2
Substitute Motif #2 for Motif #1 on A graph for 1 Front.

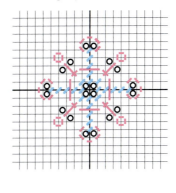

Motif #3
Substitute Motif #3 for Motif #1 on A graph for 1 Front.

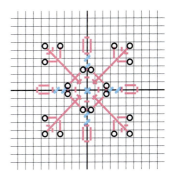

COLOR KEY
Snowflake Napkin Cuffs

	METALLIC YARN	RAINBOW GALLERY®
■	Silver 10 yds. [9.1m]	#PC2

	WORSTED-WEIGHT	RAINBOW GALLERY®
■	White Arctic Rays 10 yds. [9.1m]	#AR2

	WORSTED-WEIGHT	RED HEART CLASSIC®
□	Teal 64 yds. [58.5m]	#48
■	White 12 yds. [11m]	#1

Gobbler Pumpkin Pokes

Designed by Joan Green

Transform a pumpkin into a plump Thanksgiving turkey centerpiece.

SIZES
Body is 5" x 5¾" [12.7cm x 14.6cm]; each Feather is 2" x 6" [5.1cm x 15.2cm].

MATERIALS
• One sheet of 7-mesh plastic canvas
• Seven 1¾" [4.4cm] T-pins
• Metallic yarn (for amount see Color Key).
• Worsted-weight or plastic canvas yarn (for amounts see Color Key).

CUTTING INSTRUCTIONS
A: For Body, cut one according to graph.
B: For Feathers, cut five according to graph.

STITCHING INSTRUCTIONS
1: Using colors and stitches indicated, work pieces according to graphs; with matching colors, overcast edges of pieces.

2: Using yarn in colors and embroidery stitches indicated, embroider detail on A as indicated on graph.

3: Insert one T-pin (use two for Body) through yarn on wrong side of each piece; stick T-pins into pumpkin (see photo).

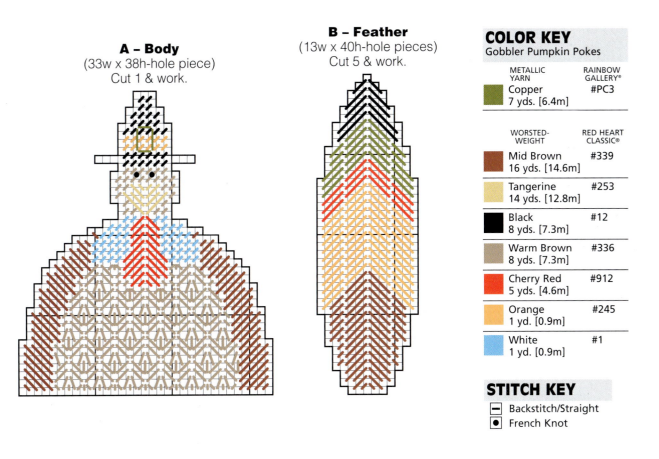

A – Body
(33w x 38h-hole piece)
Cut 1 & work.

B – Feather
(13w x 40h-hole pieces)
Cut 5 & work.

COLOR KEY
Gobbler Pumpkin Pokes

	METALLIC YARN	RAINBOW GALLERY®
🟩	Copper 7 yds. [6.4m]	#PC3

	WORSTED-WEIGHT	RED HEART CLASSIC®
🟫	Mid Brown 16 yds. [14.6m]	#339
🟨	Tangerine 14 yds. [12.8m]	#253
⬛	Black 8 yds. [7.3m]	#12
🟫	Warm Brown 8 yds. [7.3m]	#336
🟥	Cherry Red 5 yds. [4.6m]	#912
🟧	Orange 1 yd. [0.9m]	#245
🟦	White 1 yd. [0.9m]	#1

STITCH KEY
⊟ Backstitch/Straight
⊡ French Knot

Family Album

Designed by Kristine Loffredo

Keep your most treasured family photos in this inspirational display album.

SIZE
8½" x 9¼" [21.6cm x 23.5cm], not including binder.

MATERIALS
• One sheet of light blue 7-mesh plastic canvas
• One three-ring binder with clear vinyl pouchon front
• Craft cord (for amount see Color Key).
• Fine metallic braid or thread (for amounts see Color Key).

CUTTING INSTRUCTIONS
For Hearts & Cross, cut one according to graph.

STITCHING INSTRUCTIONS
1: Using colors and stitches indicated, work piece according to graph; do not overcast edges.

2: Place worked piece inside vinyl pouch of binder.

Hearts & Cross
(56w x 61h-hole piece) Cut 1 & work.
Cut out gray areas carefully.

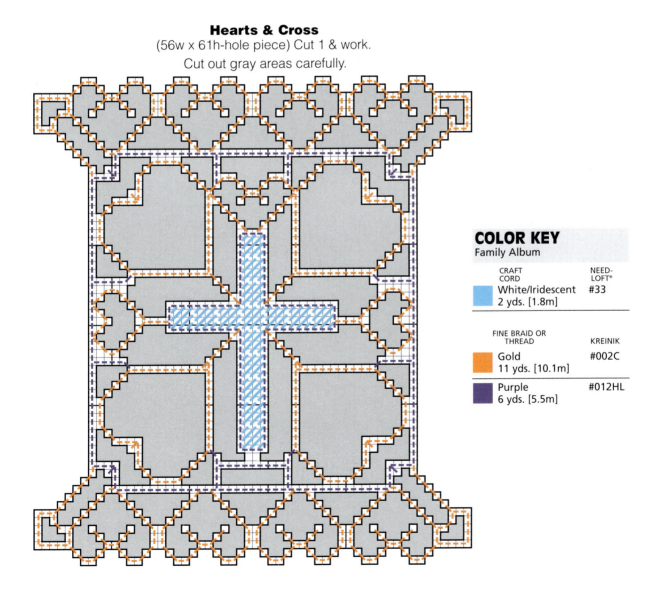

COLOR KEY
Family Album

	CRAFT CORD	NEED-LOFT®
■	White/Iridescent 2 yds. [1.8m]	#33

	FINE BRAID OR THREAD	KREINIK
■	Gold 11 yds. [10.1m]	#002C
■	Purple 6 yds. [5.5m]	#012HL

Butterfly Trivets

Designed by Mike Vickery

Protect surfaces from hot serving dishes with springtime's messengers.

SIZES

Butterfly #1 is 7½" across x 5" [19cm x 12.7cm]; Butterfly #2 is 8" across x 6½" [20.3cm x 16.5cm].

MATERIALS

• Two sheets of 7-mesh plastic canvas
• Worsted-weight or plastic canvas yarn (for amounts see Color Key).

CUTTING INSTRUCTIONS

A: For Butterfly #1 Front and Backing, cut two (one for Front and one for Backing) according to graph.

B: For Butterfly #2 Front and Backing, cut two (one for Front and one for Backing) according to graph.

STITCHING INSTRUCTIONS

NOTE: Backings are not worked.

1: Using colors indicated and continental stitch, work Front A and Front B pieces according to graphs.

2: Holding Backings to wrong side of corresponding Fronts, with black, whipstitch together. Display as desired.

A – Butterfly #1 Front & Backing
(49w x 34h-hole pieces)
Cut 2. Work 1 for Front & leave 1 unworked for Backing.

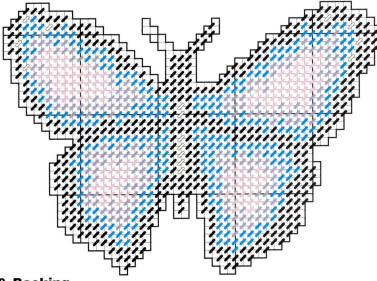

B – Butterfly #2 Front & Backing
(53w x 42h-hole pieces)
Cut 2. Work 1 for Front & leave 1 unworked for Backing.

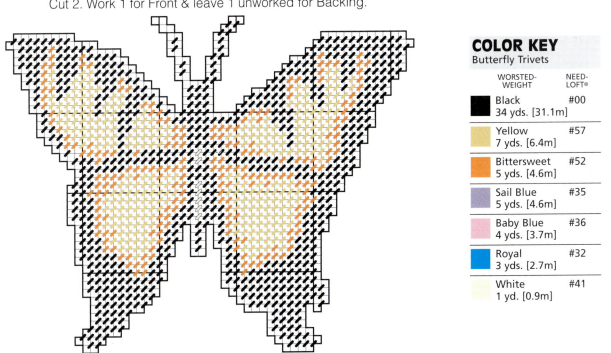

COLOR KEY
Butterfly Trivets

	WORSTED-WEIGHT	NEED-LOFT®
■ Black	34 yds. [31.1m]	#00
Yellow	7 yds. [6.4m]	#57
Bittersweet	5 yds. [4.6m]	#52
Sail Blue	5 yds. [4.6m]	#35
Baby Blue	4 yds. [3.7m]	#36
Royal	3 yds. [2.7m]	#32
White	1 yd. [0.9m]	#41

Be Mine Door Hanger

Designed by Ruby Thacker

Leave a special Valentine surprise on the door of your beloved.

SIZE
2" x 5¾" x 6" [5.1cm x 14.6cm x 15.2cm], not including hanger.

MATERIALS
- One sheet of 7-mesh plastic canvas
- Scrap piece of 10-mesh plastic canvas
- 16" [40.6cm] strand of 4mm gold pearls
- Three 6mm yellow faceted beads
- 18" [45.7cm] length of medium gauge floral wire
- Green floral tape
- 24" [61cm] length of gold-edged orchid ribbon
- Craft glue or glue gun
- Six-strand embroidery floss (for amount see Color Key on page 68).
- Worsted-weight or plastic canvas yarn (for amounts see Color Key).

CUTTING INSTRUCTIONS
NOTE: Cut A-E pieces from 7-mesh and F-J pieces from 10-mesh.

A: For Heart Front and Back, cut two (one for Front and one for Back) according to graph.
B: For Rosebud and Rose Inner Petals, cut three (one for Rosebud and two for Rose Inner Petals) according to graph.
C: For Rose Outer Petals, cut two according to graph.
D: For Calyx, cut three according to graph.
E: For Leaves, cut two according to graph.
F: For "B", cut one according to graph.
G: For "E", cut two according to graph.
H: For "M", cut one according to graph.
I: For "I", cut one according to graph.
J: For "N", cut one according to graph.

STITCHING INSTRUCTIONS
NOTE: F-I pieces are not worked.

1: Using colors and stitches indicated, work A-E pieces according to graphs; with black floss for F-J and with matching colors, overcast edges of B-J pieces.

2: Holding Front and Back A pieces wrong sides together, with orchid, whipstitch together inserting each end of 16" pearl string between Front and Back as you work (see photo).

3: For Rosebud (make 1), Inner Petals (make 2), and Calyx (make 3), with matching colors, tack individual pieces together at u holes as indicated on graphs. For Outer Petals (make 2), tack together at each #1 and opposite #2 as indicated.

NOTE: Cut floral wire into three 6" [15.2cm] lengths.

4: Assemble wire, beads and B-E pieces according to Rose Assembly Illustration. Wrap stems of Rosebud and each Rose with floral tape; shape into desired arrangement and wrap Rosebud and Rose stems together as one. Glue Leaves to stem.

5: Make a four-looped bow from ribbon and glue to stem of Roses; glue rose stem to one side of Heart and "BE MINE" letters to Heart as shown in photo.

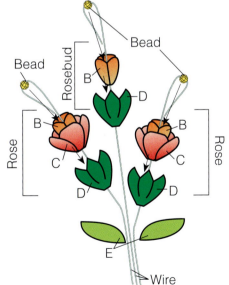

Rose Assembly Illustration
(Pieces are shown in different colors for contrast.)

A – Heart Front & Backing
(39w x 37h-hole pieces)
Cut 2 from 7-mesh & work.

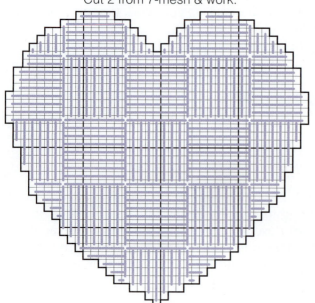

B – Rosebud & Rose Inner Petal
(13w x 7h-hole pieces)
Cut 3 from 7-mesh. Work 1 for Rosebud
& 2 for Rose Inner Petals.

With red, whipstitch X edges
together on Rosebud only.

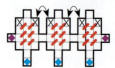

C – Rose Outer Petals
(13w x 13h-hole pieces)
Cut 2 from 7-mesh & work.

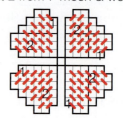

D – Calyx
(17w x 7h-hole pieces)
Cut 3 from 7-mesh & work.

E – Leaf
(6w x 6h-hole pieces)
Cut 2 from 7-mesh & work.

F – "B"
(4w x 7h-hole piece)
Cut 1 from 10-mesh.
Cut out gray areas.

G – "E"
(4w x 7h-hole pieces)
Cut 2 from 10-mesh.

H – "M"
(7w x 7h-hole piece)
Cut 1 from 10-mesh.

I – "I"
(3w x 7h-hole piece)
Cut 1 from 10-mesh.

J – "N"
(5w x 7h-hole piece)
Cut 1 from 10-mesh & work.

COLOR KEY
Be Mine Door Hanger

	EMBROIDERY FLOSS	
■	Black 6 yds. [5.5m]	

	WORSTED-WEIGHT	NEED-LOFT®
	Orchid 22 yds. [20.1m]	#44
	Red 10 yds. [9.1m]	#01
	Holly 6 yds. [5.5m]	#27

Heavenly Trio

Designed by Joan Green

Celebrate the season with a chorus of angels for the tree.

SIZE
Each is about 2" x 5" x 6" tall [5.1cm x 12.7cm x 15.2cm], not including hanger.

MATERIALS
- One sheet of 7-mesh plastic canvas
- Three 18.5 x 18mm faceted heart-shaped gemstones (one purple, one lt. blue and one fuchsia)
- 18" [45.7cm] length of gold glitter stem
- Three 27" [69cm] lengths of 1¼" [3.2cm] wire-edged ribbon in colors of choice
- Craft glue or glue gun
- Metallic yarn (for amounts see Color Key).
- Worsted-weight or plastic canvas yarn (for amounts see Color Key).

CUTTING INSTRUCTIONS
A: For Angel #1-#3 Bodies, cut one each according to graphs.

B: For Angel #1-#3 Arms, cut one each according to graphs.

STITCHING INSTRUCTIONS
1: Using colors and stitches indicated, work pieces according to graphs; omitting attachment areas, with matching colors as shown in photo, overcast edges of pieces.

NOTES: Cut each 27" length of ribbon into three equal 9" [22.9cm] lengths. Cut glitter stem into six 3" [7.6cm] lengths.

2: Whipstitch and assemble corresponding A and B pieces, ribbons, gemstones and glitter stems according to Angel Assembly Diagram.

3: Hang or display as desired.

A – Angel #1 Body
(9w x 15h-hole piece)
Cut 1 & work.

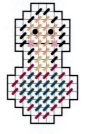

B – Angel #1 Arm
(31w x 17h-hole piece)
Cut 1 & work.

A – Angel #3 Body
(9w x 15h-hole piece)
Cut 1 & work.

B – Angel #2 Arm
(31w x 17h-hole piece)
Cut 1 & work.

A – Angel #2 Body
(9w x 15h-hole piece)
Cut 1 & work.

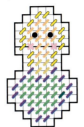

B – Angel #3 Arm
(31w x 17h-hole piece)
Cut 1 & work.

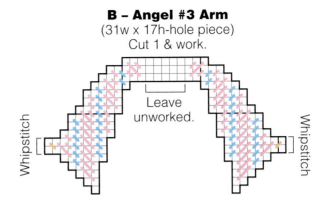

Whipstitch

Leave unworked.

Whipstitch

COLOR KEY
Heavenly Trio

	METALLIC YARN	RAINBOW GALLERY®
▮	Fuchsia 2 yds. [1.8m]	#PC13
▮	Lt. Blue 2 yds. [1.8m]	#PC14
▮	Purple 2 yds. [1.8m]	#PC15

	WORSTED-WEIGHT	RED HEART CLASSIC®
▮	Lt. Teal 4 yds. [3.7m]	#355
▮	Med. Teal 4 yds. [3.7m]	#359
▮	Rose Pink 4 yds. [3.7m]	#372
▮	Honey Gold 1 yd. [0.9m]	#645
▮	Mid Brown 1 yd. [0.9m]	#339
▮	Peach 1 yd. [0.9m]	#325
▮	Warm Brown 1 yd. [0.9m]	#336

STITCH KEY
⊡ French Knot

Angel Assembly Diagram
(Gray denotes wrong side.)

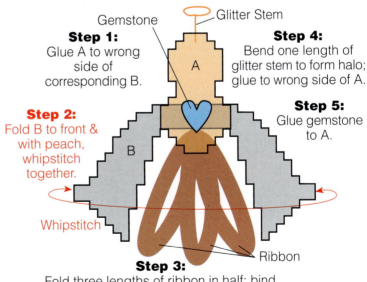

Gemstone

Glitter Stem

Step 1:
Glue A to wrong side of corresponding B.

Step 4:
Bend one length of glitter stem to form halo; glue to wrong side of A.

Step 2:
Fold B to front & with peach, whipstitch together.

Step 5:
Glue gemstone to A.

Whipstitch

Ribbon

Step 3:
Fold three lengths of ribbon in half; bind ends together using one length of glitter stem & glue to wrong side of B.

Bargello Tissue Cover

Designed by Joan Green

Learn a time-honored bargello flame stitch pattern and create a lovely gift.

SIZE
Loosely covers a boutique-style tissue box.

MATERIALS
- Two sheets of 7-mesh plastic canvas
- Velcro® closure (optional)
- Craft glue or glue gun (optional)
- Metallic cord (for amount see Color Key).
- Worsted-weight or plastic canvas yarn
  (for amounts see Color Key).

CUTTING INSTRUCTIONS
A: For Sides, cut four 31w x 37h-holes.

B: For Top, cut one according to graph.

C: For Optional Bottom and Flap, cut one 31w x 31h-holes for Bottom and one 12w x 31h-holes for Flap (no graphs).

STITCHING INSTRUCTIONS
NOTE: C pieces are not worked.

1: Using colors and stitches indicated, work A and B pieces according to graphs.

2: With tan, whipstitch A and B pieces wrong sides together, forming Cover. For Optional Bottom, whipstitch C pieces together and to one Cover Side according to Optional Bottom Assembly Illustration. Overcast unfinished edges of Cover. Glue closure to Flap and inside Cover (see illustration).

Optional Tissue Cover Bottom Assembly Illustration

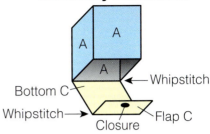

COLOR KEY
Bargello Tissue Cover

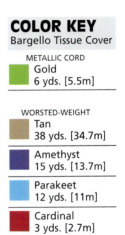

	METALLIC CORD	
🟩	Gold	6 yds. [5.5m]

	WORSTED-WEIGHT	
🟫	Tan	38 yds. [34.7m]
🟪	Amethyst	15 yds. [13.7m]
🟦	Parakeet	12 yds. [11m]
🟥	Cardinal	3 yds. [2.7m]

B – Top
(31w x 31h-hole piece)
Cut 1 & work.

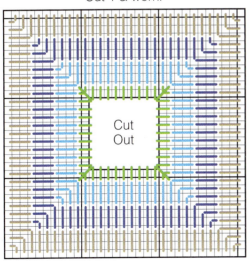

A – Side
(31w x 37h-hole pieces)
Cut 4 & work.

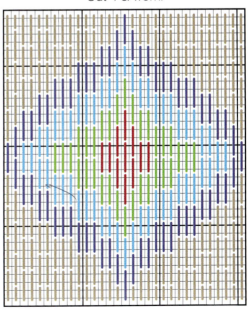

Sports Straws

Designed by Darlene Neubauer

Little ones will love using these clever straws
to cool off after ball games.

SIZE
Each Motif is about 2¼" x 2¼" [5.7cm x 5.7cm], not including straw.

MATERIALS
• One sheet of 7-mesh plastic canvas
• Eight plastic flex straws
• Worsted-weight or plastic canvas yarn
  (for amounts see Color Key).

CUTTING INSTRUCTIONS
A: For Baseball, cut two according to graph.
B: For Golf Ball, cut two according to graph.
C: For Football, cut two according to graph.
D: For Tennis Ball, cut two according to graph.
E: For Basketball, cut two according to graph.
F: For Soccer Ball, cut two according to graph.
G: For Volleyball, cut two according to graph.

H: For Bowling Ball, cut two according to graph.

STITCHING INSTRUCTIONS
1: Using colors indicated and continental stitch, work pieces according to graphs.

2: With black (Separate into individual plies, if desired.) and backstitch, embroider detail on F pieces as indicated on graph.

3: With white for Baseball, Golf Ball, Soccer Ball and Volleyball and with matching colors, whipstitch corresponding pieces wrong sides together as indicated. Overcast unfinished edges.

4: Insert one straw through each Motif (see photo).

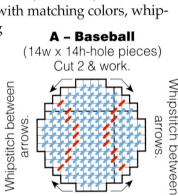

A – Baseball
(14w x 14h-hole pieces)
Cut 2 & work.
Whipstitch between arrows.

COLOR KEY
Sports Straws

WORSTED-WEIGHT

■ (blue)	White 15 yds. [13.7m]
■ (black)	Black 6 yds. [5.5m]
■ (brown)	Medium Brown 5 yds. [4.6m]
■ (gray)	Gray 4 yds. [3.7m]
■ (yellow)	Yellow 4 yds. [3.7m]
■ (orange)	Orange 3 yds. [2.7m]
■ (red)	Red 1 yd. [0.9m]

STITCH KEY
⊟ Backstitch/Straight

C – Football
(18w x 12h-hole pieces)
Cut 2 & work.
Whipstitch between arrows.

B – Golf Ball
(14w x 14h-hole pieces)
Cut 2 & work.
Whipstitch between arrows.

D – Tennis Ball
(14w x 14h-hole pieces)
Cut 2 & work.
Whipstitch between arrows.

E – Basketball
(14w x 14h-hole pieces)
Cut 2 & work.
Whipstitch between arrows.

F – Soccer Ball
(14w x 14h-hole pieces)
Cut 2 & work.
Whipstitch between arrows.

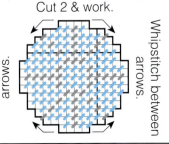

G – Volleyball
(14w x 14h-hole pieces)
Cut 2 & work.
Whipstitch between arrows.

H – Bowling Ball
(14w x 14h-hole pieces)
Cut 2 & work.
Whipstitch between arrows.

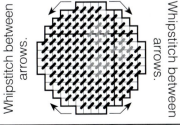

Ghostly Surprises

Designed by Linda McGinnis

Each little ghost holds candy or a little party favor.

SIZE
Each is 1⅞" across x 3¼" tall [4.8cm x 8.3cm] when assembled.

MATERIALS
- One sheet of 7-mesh plastic canvas
- Six ½" [13mm] orange pom-poms
- Craft glue or glue gun
- Worsted-weight or plastic canvas yarn (for amounts see Color Key).

CUTTING INSTRUCTIONS
A: For Cup Tops and Bottoms, cut twelve (six for Tops and six for Bottoms) according to graph.

B: For Cup Sides, cut six 41w x 8h-holes.

C: For Ghost Bodies, cut six according to graph.

D: For Ghost Arms, cut twelve 4w x 2h-holes.

E: For Ghost Legs, cut twelve according to graph.

F: For Bow Ties, cut six according to graph.

STITCHING INSTRUCTIONS
NOTE: Bottom A pieces are not worked.

1: Using colors and stitches indicated, work Top A, B (overlap ends as indicated on graph and work through both thicknesses at overlap area to join) and C-F pieces according to graphs. Omitting attachment areas, with matching colors, overcast edges of C-F pieces.

2: For each Cup (make 6), with tangerine, whipstitch one Top A, one Bottom A and one B together according to Cup Assembly Illustration; overcast unfinished edges.

3: For each Ghost (make 6), with white, whipstitch two D and two E pieces to one C as indicated on graphs.

NOTE: Thread a 6" [15.2cm] length of paddy green through needle.

4: For each stemmed pumpkin (make 6), knot end of thread and insert needle through one pom-pom and pull yarn through to opposite side; clip end of yarn to ¼" [6mm] (see photo).

5: Glue one Bow Tie to each Ghost; glue one Ghost and one Pumpkin to Top of each Cup as shown.

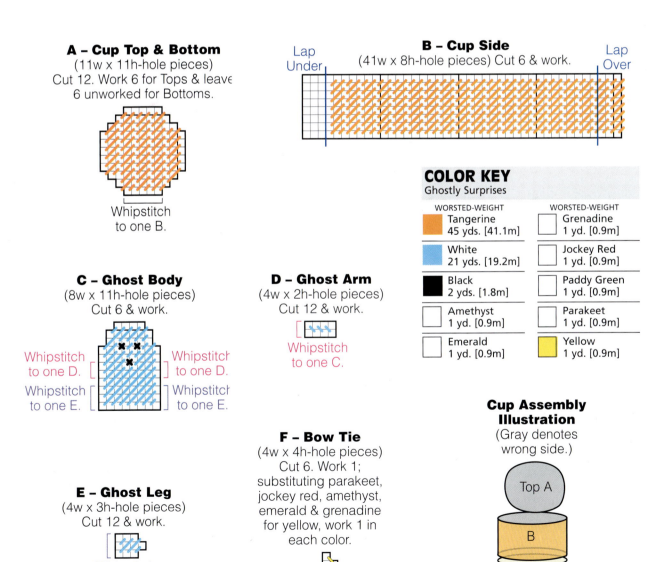

A – Cup Top & Bottom
(11w x 11h-hole pieces)
Cut 12. Work 6 for Tops & leave 6 unworked for Bottoms.

Whipstitch to one B.

B – Cup Side
(41w x 8h-hole pieces) Cut 6 & work.
Lap Under
Lap Over

COLOR KEY
Ghostly Surprises

WORSTED-WEIGHT	WORSTED-WEIGHT
Tangerine 45 yds. [41.1m]	Grenadine 1 yd. [0.9m]
White 21 yds. [19.2m]	Jockey Red 1 yd. [0.9m]
Black 2 yds. [1.8m]	Paddy Green 1 yd. [0.9m]
Amethyst 1 yd. [0.9m]	Parakeet 1 yd. [0.9m]
Emerald 1 yd. [0.9m]	Yellow 1 yd. [0.9m]

C – Ghost Body
(8w x 11h-hole pieces)
Cut 6 & work.

Whipstitch to one D.
Whipstitch to one D.
Whipstitch to one E.
Whipstitch to one E.

D – Ghost Arm
(4w x 2h-hole pieces)
Cut 12 & work.

Whipstitch to one C.

E – Ghost Leg
(4w x 3h-hole pieces)
Cut 12 & work.

Whipstitch to one C.

F – Bow Tie
(4w x 4h-hole pieces)
Cut 6. Work 1; substituting parakeet, jockey red, amethyst, emerald & grenadine for yellow, work 1 in each color.

Cup Assembly Illustration
(Gray denotes wrong side.)

Top A
B
Bottom A

Santa Door Hanger

Designed by Michele Wilcox

Welcome guests with a stylized Santa door hanger.

SIZE
7½" x 13" [19cm x 33cm].

MATERIALS
• One sheet of 7-mesh plastic canvas
• No. 5 pearl cotton [coton perlé]
  (for amounts see Color Key).
• Worsted-weight or plastic canvas
  yarn (for amounts see Color Key).

CUTTING INSTRUCTIONS
For Santa, cut one according
to graph.

STITCHING INSTRUCTIONS
1: Using colors indicated and continental stitch, work piece according
to graph; with matching colors,
overcast edges.

2: Using pearl cotton in colors and embroidery
stitches indicated, embroider detail on piece as
indicated on graph.

3: Hang as desired.

Santa
(48w x 85h-hole piece)
Cut 1 & work.

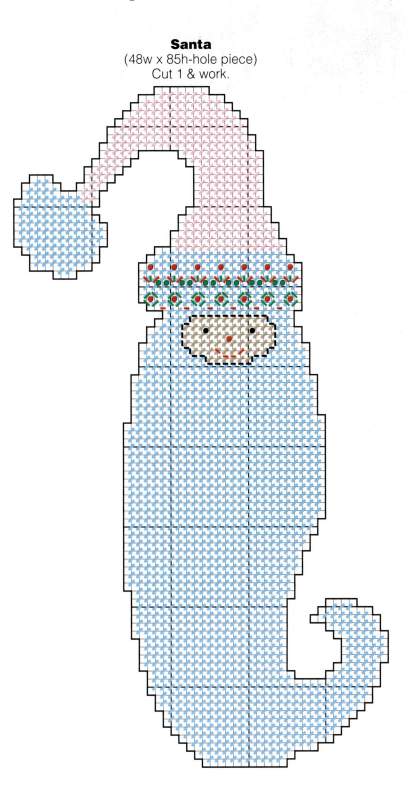

COLOR KEY
Santa Door Hanger

NO. 5
PEARL COTTON

■	Green	2 yds. [1.8m]
■	Red	2 yds. [1.8m]
■	Black	1 yd. [0.9m]

	WORSTED-WEIGHT	NEED-LOFT®
■	Eggshell 32 yds. [29.3m]	#39
■	Red 5 yds. [4.6m]	#01
■	Beige 2 yds. [1.8m]	#40

Friends Forever

Designed by Debbie Tabor

Share memories of carefree times with a frame stitched with friendship motifs.

SIZE
Motif is 5¼" x 6" [13.3cm x 15.2cm].

MATERIALS
- ½ sheet of 7-mesh plastic canvas
- One basket of choice
- Two 18" [45.7cm] lengths of ivory twisted craft paper
- One 18" [45.7cm] length of dk. red and tan twisted craft paper
- Three 18" [45.7cm] lengths of raffia straw
- Craft glue or glue gun
- No. 3 pearl cotton (coton perlé) (for amounts see Color Key)
- No. 5 pearl cotton (coton perlé) (for amount see Color Key)
- Worsted-weight or plastic canvas yarn (for amounts see Color Key).

CUTTING INSTRUCTIONS
For Butterfly Motif, cut one according to graph.

STITCHING INSTRUCTIONS
1: Using colors and stitches indicated, work piece according to graph; with matching colors as shown in photo, overcast edges of piece.

2: Using pearl cotton in colors and embroidery stitches indicated, embroider detail on piece as indicated on graph.

NOTE: *Cut one 2½" [6.4cm] and one 1" [2.5cm] length of No. 5 pearl cotton.*

3: For large Butterfly antennae, using 2½" length, from back to front, insert each end through one hole as indicated, glue to secure. For small Butterfly antennae, glue 1" length of pearl cotton to wrong side of Motif at hole as shown in photo. Glue to secure.

4: Untwist craft paper, shape ivory craft paper into two loops; shape dk. red and tan craft paper into a bow. Glue loops on top of Bow. Tie each raffia length into a bow and glue to top of craft paper assembly (see photo). Glue Butterfly to center of craft paper assembly and assembly to basket.

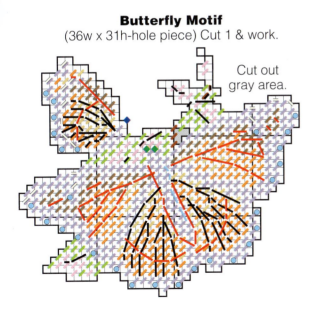

Butterfly Motif
(36w x 31h-hole piece) Cut 1 & work.

Cut out gray area.

COLOR KEY
Butterfly Motif Basket

NO. 3 PEARL COTTON	DMC®		WORSTED-WEIGHT	NEED-LOFT®
Black 2 yds. [1.8m]	#310		Moss 2 yds. [1.8m]	#25
White 2 yds. [1.8m]			Rust 2 yds. [1.8m]	#09
NO. 5 PEARL COTTON	**DMC®**		Tangerine 2 yds. [1.8m]	#11
Black 4 yds. [3.7m]	#310		Camel 1 yd. [0.9m]	#43
WORSTED-WEIGHT	**NEED-LOFT®**		Silver 1 yd. [0.9m]	#37
Black 6 yds. [5.5m]	#00		White 1 yd. [1.9m]	#41
Pumpkin 4 yds. [3.7m]	#12			

STITCH KEY
- — Backstitch/Straight
- ● French Knot

B – "Friends" Motif
(27w x 8h-hole piece)
Cut 1 from 10-mesh & work.

C – "Forever" Motif
(26w x 8h-hole piece)
Cut 1 from 10-mesh & work.

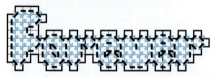

COLOR KEY
Friends Forever Frame

EMBROIDERY FLOSS	DMC®	EMBROIDERY FLOSS	DMC®
■ Black 4 yds. [3.7m]	#310	■ Bt. Red ½ yd. [0.5m]	#666
■ Delft Blue 4 yds. [3.7m]	#809	■ Dk. Cyclamen Pink ½ yd. [0.5m]	#3804
■ Lemon 2 yds. [1.8m]	#307	■ Lt. Seagreen ½ yd. [0.5m]	#964
□ Lt. Cyclamen Pink 1 yd. [0.9m]	#3806	■ Med. Aquamarine ½ yd. [0.5m]	#943
■ Lt. Parrot Green 1 yd. [0.9m]	#907	■ Violet ½ yd. [0.5m]	#553
■ Apricot ½ yd. [0.5m]	#3341	WORSTED-WEIGHT	
■ Bt. Orange-Red ½ yd. [0.5m]	#606	■ Gray 15 yds. [13.7m]	

STITCH KEY

⊟ Backstitch/Straight

D – Smile Motif
(10w x 10h-hole pieces)
Cut 2 from 10-mesh. Work 1; substituting lt. cyclamen pink for lemon, work 1.

E – Heart Motif
(8w x 8h-hole piece)
Cut 1 from 10-mesh & work.

F – Peace Motif
(10w x 10h-hole piece)
Cut 1 from 10-mesh & work.

G – Flower #1
(10w x 10h-hole piece)
Cut 1 from 10-mesh & work.

G – Flower #2
(10w x 10h-hole piece)
Cut 1 from 10-mesh & work.

G – Flower #3
(10w x 10h-hole piece)
Cut 1 from 10-mesh & work.

Tea Light Lamp Shades

Designed by Kristine Loffredo

These clever lamp shades will set the holiday mood.

SIZE

Each is about 6¼" across x 2" tall [15.9cm x 5.1cm], not including embellishments.

MATERIALS FOR ONE

- ½ sheet of 7-mesh plastic canvas
- One 9" [8.2cm] plastic canvas circle
- One wine glass
- One tea light candle
- Six 5" [12.7cm] lengths of raffia straw
- Craft glue or glue gun
- Craft cord (for amounts see individual Color Keys)
- Worsted-weight or plastic canvas yarn (for amounts see individual Color Keys).

CUTTING INSTRUCTIONS

A: For Shade, cut one from circle according to graph of choice.

B: For Butterfly Shade Flowers, cut four according to graph.

C: For Butterfly Shade Wings #1 and #2, cut two each according to graphs.

D: For Candy Corn Shade Bat #1, cut one according to graph.

E: For Candy Corn Shade Bat #2, cut one according to graph.

F: For Candy Corn Shade Candies, cut four according to graph.

G: For Fourth of July Shade Stars, cut five according to graph.

H: For Acorn Shade Leaves, cut two according to graph.

I: For Acorn Shade Acorn Cap, cut four according to graph.

J: For Acorn Shade Nut, cut four according to graph.

STITCHING INSTRUCTIONS:

1: Using colors and stitches indicated, work pieces according to graphs of choice. With iridescent yellow cord for Butterfly Shade, blue cord for Candy Corn Shade, burgundy for Acorn Shade and with matching colors, overcast edges of A, B and D-J pieces.

2: With black and embroidery stitches indicated, embroider detail on C pieces as indicated on graph.

3: For Butterfly Shade Butterflies, with cinnamon, whipstitch corresponding color C pieces right sides together as indicated. With matching colors, overcast unfinished edges.

4: Glue three lengths of raffia straw to wrong side of each D and E pieces (see photo).

5: For Acorns, glue one I to top of each J piece (see photo); glue two Acorns to center of each H piece.

6: Glue Butterflies, Flowers, Candy Corn, Bats, Stars, Leaves and Acorns to corresponding Shades (see photos).

7: Place tea light candle inside wine glass; place shade on top of wine glass as shown.

COLOR KEY
Butterfly Shade

	CRAFT CORD		NEED-LOFT®
	Iridescent Yellow 3 yds. [2.7m]		#47

	WORSTED-WEIGHT		NEED-LOFT®
	Fern 16 yds. [14.6m]		#23
	Bright Purple 4 yds. [3.7m]		#64
	Burgundy 4 yds. [3.7m]		#03
	White 4 yds. [3.7m]		#41
	Lilac 2 yds. [1.8m]		#45
	Pink 2 yds. [1.8m]		#07
	Black 1 yd. [0.9m]		#00
	Cinnamon 1 yd. [0.9m]		#14

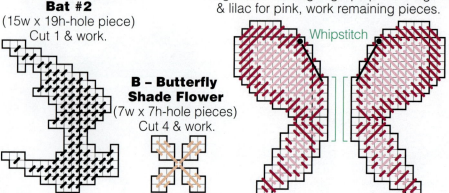

E – Candy Corn Shade Bat #2
(15w x 19h-hole piece)
Cut 1 & work.

B – Butterfly Shade Flower
(7w x 7h-hole pieces)
Cut 4 & work.

C – Butterfly Shade Wings #1 & #2
(12w x 22h-hole pieces)
Cut 2 each. Work 1 for Wing #1; work 1 for Wing #2, substituting bright purple for burgundy & lilac for pink, work remaining pieces.

Whipstitch

STITCH KEY
▬ Backstitch/Straight
⦿ French Knot

F – Candy Corn Shade Candy
(9w x 9h-hole pieces)
Cut 4 & work.

Candy Corn Shade Bat #1
(19w x 17h-hole piece)
Cut 1 & work.

A – Butterfly Shade & Candy Corn Shade
(9" circle)
Cut 2. Work 1 for Butterfly Shade; substituting
lilac for fern, work 1 for Candy Corn Shade.
Continue established pattern around each entire piece,
overlapping yellow area & working through both thicknesses
at overlap area to join.

COLOR KEY
Candy Corn Shade

	CRAFT CORD	NEED-LOFT®
	Blue 3 yds. [2.7m]	#02

	WORSTED-WEIGHT	NEED-LOFT®
	Lilac 15 yds. [13.7m]	#45
	Black 6 yds. [5.5m]	#00
	Bittersweet 2 yds. [1.8m]	#52
	Tangerine 2 yds. [1.8m]	#11
	White 1 yd. [0.9m]	#41

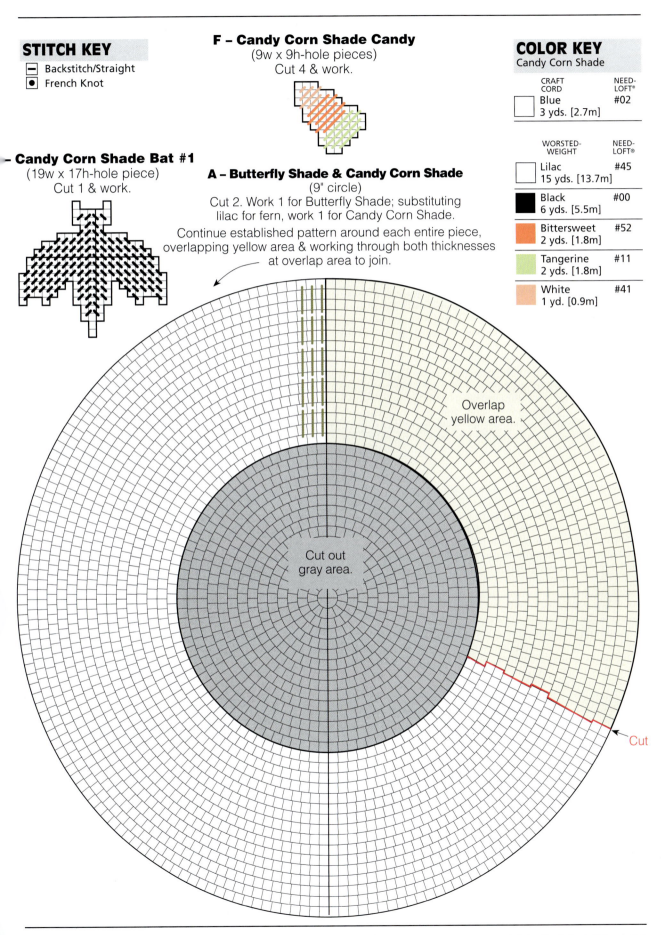

Overlap yellow area.

Cut out gray area.

Cut

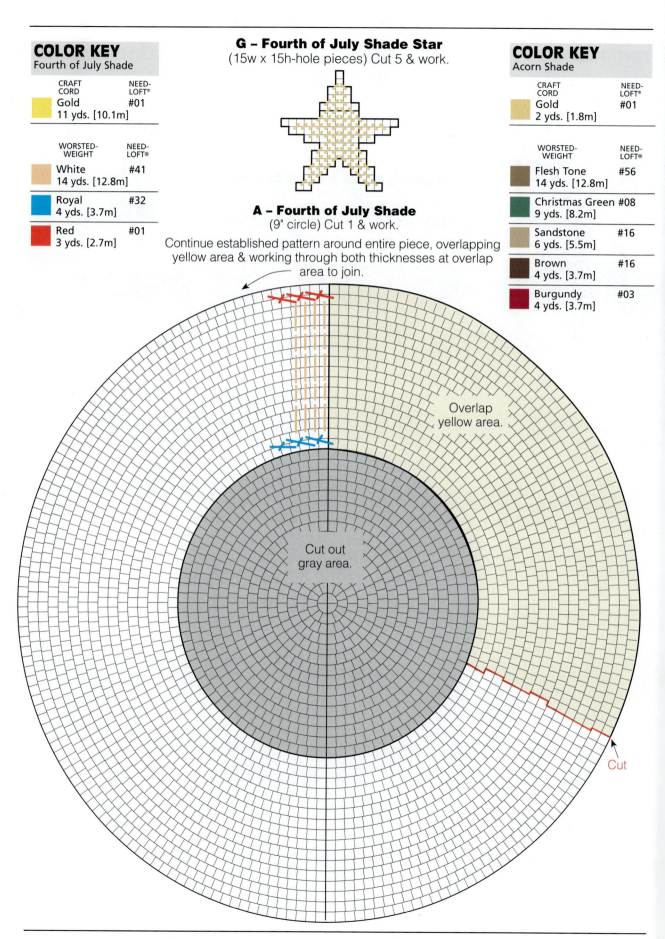

G – Fourth of July Shade Star
(15w x 15h-hole pieces) Cut 5 & work.

A – Fourth of July Shade
(9" circle) Cut 1 & work.

Continue established pattern around entire piece, overlapping yellow area & working through both thicknesses at overlap area to join.

Overlap yellow area.

Cut out gray area.

Cut

J – Acorn Shade Nut
(9w x 9h-hole pieces)
Cut 4 & work.

I – Acorn Shade Acorn Cap
(10w x 8h-hole pieces)
Cut 4 & work.

H – Acorn Shade Leaves
(30w x 30h-hole pieces)
Cut 2 & work.

A – Acorn Shade
(9" circle) Cut 1 & work.

Continue established pattern around entire piece, overlapping yellow area & working through both thicknesses at overlap area to join.

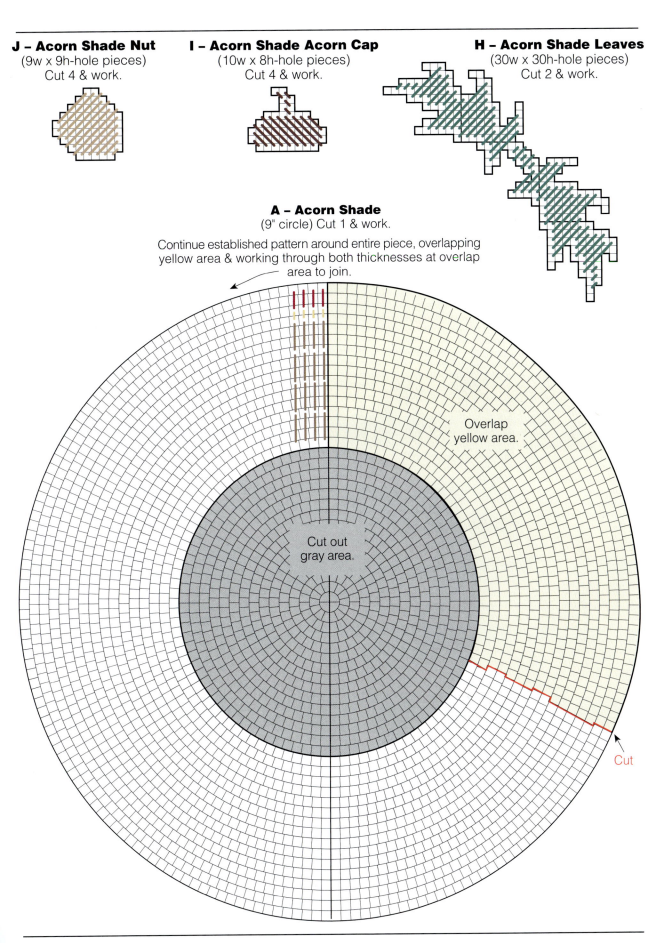

Overlap yellow area.

Cut out gray area.

Cut

Frightful Witch

Designed by Michele Wilcox

A boo-tiful witch with her friend the spider smiles from a cheery tissue cover.

SIZE
Loosely covers a boutique-style tissue box.

MATERIALS
- Two sheets of 7-mesh plastic canvas;
- Velcro® closure (optional);
- Craft glue or glue gun;
- Heavy metallic braid (for amount see Color Key);
- No. 3 pearl cotton (coton perlé) (for amounts see Color Key);
- Worsted-weight or plastic canvas yarn (for amounts see Color Key).

CUTTING INSTRUCTIONS
A: For Top, cut one according to graph.
B: For Sides, cut four 30w x 36h-holes.
C: For Optional Tissue Cover Bottom and Flap, cut one 30w x 30h-holes for Bottom and one 30w x 12h-holes for Flap (no graphs).

STITCHING INSTRUCTIONS
NOTE: C pieces are not worked.
1: Using colors indicated and continental stitch, work A and B pieces according to graphs; with rust, overcast cutout edges of A.

2: Using braid and pearl cotton in colors and embroidery stitches indicated, embroider detail on A and B pieces as indicated on graphs.

3: With rust, whipstitch A and B pieces together, forming Cover.

4: For Optional Bottom, with rust, whipstitch C pieces together and to one Cover Side according to Optional Tissue Cover Bottom Assembly Illustration; overcast unfinished edges. Glue closure to Flap and inside Cover (see illustration).

A – Top
(30w x 30h-hole piece) Cut 1 & work.

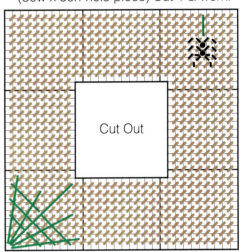

B – Side
(30w x 36h-hole pieces) Cut 4 & work.

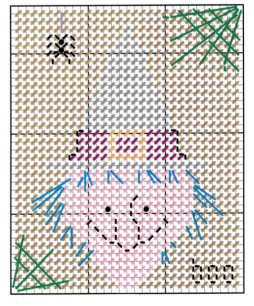

STITCH KEY
- ⊟ Backstitch/Straight
- ⊡ French Knot

Optional Tissue Cover Bottom Assembly Illustration

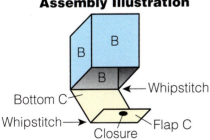

Bottom C
Whipstitch →
Closure
Whipstitch
Flap C

COLOR KEY
Frightful Witch

METALLIC BRAID	KREINIK
▦ Silver 10 yds. [9.1m]	#001

NO. 3 PEARL COTTON	
■ Black 5 yds. [4.6m]	
■ Dk. Gray 5 yds. [4.6m]	

WORSTED-WEIGHT	NEED-LOFT®
▦ Rust 26 yds. [23.8m]	#09
▦ Beige 20 yds. [18.3m]	#40
▦ Black 18 yds. [16.5m]	#00
▦ Bright Purple 18 yds. [16.5m]	#64
▦ Tangerine 1 yd. [0.9m]	#11

Pocket Tissue Holder

Designed by Michele Wilcox

Never be without a tissue with this clever tissue holder.

SIZE

3⅞" x 5¾" [9.8cm x 14.6cm], not including ribbon.

MATERIALS

• ½ sheet of 7-mesh plastic canvas
• ½ yd. [0.5m] of ¼" [6mm] decorative ribbon of choice
• No. 5 pearl cotton (coton perlé) (for amount see Color Key)
• Worsted-weight or plastic canvas yarn (for amounts see Color Key).

CUTTING INSTRUCTIONS

A: For Front, cut one according to graph.
B: For Back, cut one according to graph.

STITCHING INSTRUCTIONS

1: Using colors and stitches indicated, work pieces according to graphs; with mermaid, overcast cutouts on A and B pieces.

2: Using pearl cotton and embroidery stitches indicated, embroider detail on Front as indicated on graph.

3: With mermaid, whipstitch pieces wrong sides together as indicated; overcast unfinished top edges.

4: Insert ribbon through cutouts and tie into a bow (see photo).

A – Front
(37w x 25h-hole piece) Cut 1 & work.
Cut out gray area.

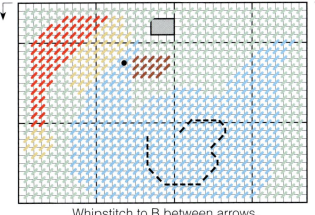

Whipstitch to B between arrows.

B – Back
(37w x 25h-hole piece) Cut 1 & work.
Cut out gray area.

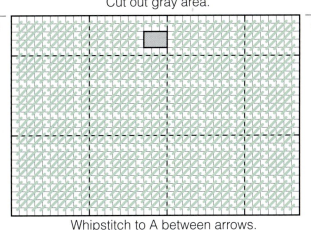

Whipstitch to A between arrows.

COLOR KEY
Pocket Tissue Holder

	NO. 5 PEARL COTTON	DMC®
■	Black 1 yd. [0.9m]	#310

	WORSTED-WEIGHT	NEED-LOFT®
	Mermaid 26 yds. [23.8m]	#53
	White 9 yds. [8.2m]	#41
	Beige 1 yd. [0.9m]	#40
	Red 1 yd. [0.9m]	#01
	Tangerine 1 yd. [0.9m]	#11

STITCH KEY

☐ Backstitch/Straight
⊙ French Knot

St. Nick Tissue Cover

Designed by Michele Wilcox

Let St. Nick decorate your room this holiday by keeping tissues within reach.

SIZE
Loosely covers a boutique-style tissue box.

MATERIALS
- Two sheets of 7-mesh plastic canvas
- Velcro® closure (optional)
- Craft glue or glue gun
- No. 5 pearl cotton (for amounts see Color Key);
- Worsted-weight or plastic canvas yarn (for amounts see Color Key).

CUTTING INSTRUCTIONS
A: For Sides, cut four 30w x 36h-holes.
B: For Top, cut one according to graph.
C: For Optional Tissue Cover Bottom and Flap, cut one 30w x 30h-holes for Bottom and one 30w x 12h-holes for Flap (no graphs).

STITCHING INSTRUCTIONS
NOTE: C pieces are not worked.

1: Using colors and stitches indicated, work pieces according to graphs; with red, overcast cutout edges of B.

2: Using pearl cotton in colors and embroidery stitches indicated, embroider detail on A pieces as indicated on graph.

3: With red, whipstitch A and B pieces together, forming Cover.

4: For Optional Bottom, with Christmas red, whipstitch C pieces together and to one Cover Side according to Optional Tissue Cover Bottom Assembly Illustration; overcast unfinished edges. Glue closure to Flap and inside Cover (see illustration).

A – Side
(30w x 36h-hole pieces) Cut 4 & work.

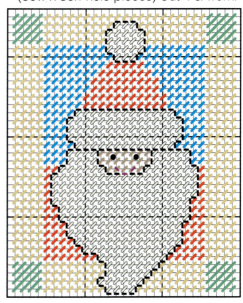

STITCH KEY
- ─ Backstitch/Straight
- ● French Knot

COLOR KEY
St. Nick Tissue Cover

NO. 5 PEARL COTTON	DMC®
■ Black 8 yds. [7.3m]	#310
■ Bright Red 1 yd. [0.9m]	#666

WORSTED-WEIGHT	NEED-LOFT®
Yellow 36 yds. [32.9m]	#57
White 24 yds. [21.9m]	#41
Bright Blue 20 yds. [18.3m]	#60
Christmas Red 20 yds. [18.3m]	#02
Christmas Green 6 yds. [5.5m]	#28
Beige 2 yds. [1.8m]	#40

Optional Tissue Cover Bottom Assembly Illustration

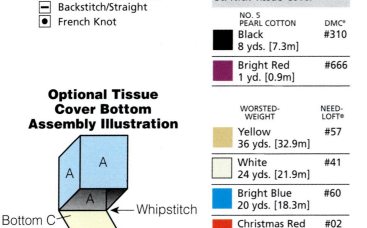

Bottom C
Whipstitch
Closure
Whipstitch
Flap C
A A A A

B – Top
(30w x 30h-hole piece) Cut 1 & work.

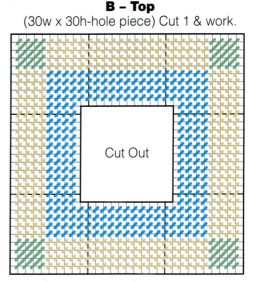

Cut Out

Patriotic Plant Poke

Designed by Laura Victory

Display the red, white and blue year-round with this star-shaped plant poke.

SIZE
5½" x 18½" [14cm x 47cm].

MATERIALS
- One 5" [12.7cm] plastic canvas star shape
- 18" [45.7cm] length of ¼" [6mm] dowel
- White paint and paint brush
- Five assorted buttons (2 blue, 2 red and 1 white)
- ⅔ yd. [0.6m] length of white ¼" [6mm] satin ribbon;
- ⅔ yd. [0.6cm] length of red decorative star wire garland
- Craft glue or glue gun;
- Worsted-weight or plastic canvas yarn (for amounts see Color Key).

CUTTING INSTRUCTIONS
For Patriotic Star, use one star shape.

STITCHING INSTRUCTIONS
1: Using colors and stitches indicated, work piece according to graph; with matching colors, overcast edges.

NOTE: *Cut ribbon into one 3" [7.6cm], one 5" [12.7cm], one 7" [17.8cm] and one 9" [22.9cm] length.*

2: Glue end of each length to wrong side of Star at each point (see photo); glue one button to opposite end of each length. Glue remaining button to center of Star.

NOTE: *Paint dowel; let dry.*

3: Glue dowel to wrong side of Star; wrap garland around dowel as shown. Display as desired.

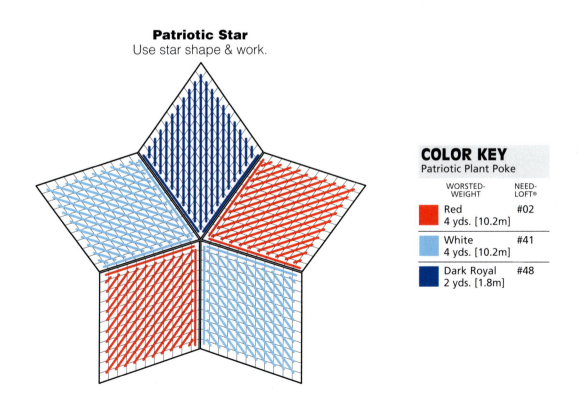

Patriotic Star
Use star shape & work.

COLOR KEY
Patriotic Plant Poke

	WORSTED-WEIGHT	NEED-LOFT®
Red 4 yds. [10.2m]		#02
White 4 yds. [10.2m]		#41
Dark Royal 2 yds. [1.8m]		#48

Butterfly Trio

Designed by Carol Krob

Create a wonderful gift while having fun stitching
with sparkly metallic yarns and jewels.

SIZES

Small Butterfly is 4½" x 4¾" [11.4cm x 12.1cm]; Medium Butterfly is 5½" x 6" [14cm x 15.2cm]; Large Butterfly is 7" x 7¾" [17.8cm x 19.7cm].

MATERIALS

- Two sheets of 7-mesh plastic canvas
- Six 2" [5.1cm] pearl head pins
- 20 Victorian Gold, 20 Silver and 20 Copper glass seed beads
- Two pink 10 x 7mm, two turquoise 10 x 7mm, two dark fuchsia 10 x 7mm and two emerald 10 x 7mm flat-backed pear-shaped cabochons
- Two pink 13 x 9mm, two turquoise 13 x 9mm, two dark fuchsia 13 x 9mm and two 13 x 9mm flat-backed pear-shaped cabochons
- Two pink 15 x 11mm, two turquoise 15 x 11mm and two dark fuchsia 15 x 11mm flat-backed pear-shaped cabochons, two 18 x 8mm emerald flat-backed teardrop cabochons
- Craft glue or glue gun
- Metallic yarn (for amounts see Color Key).

CUTTING INSTRUCTIONS

A: For Small Butterfly, cut one according to graph.

B: For Medium Butterfly, cut one according to graph.

C: For Large Butterfly, cut one according to graph.

STITCHING INSTRUCTIONS:

1: Using colors and stitches indicated, work pieces according to graphs; with dark gold for Small Butterfly, Bronze for Medium Butterfly and Pewter for Large Butterfly, overcast edges of A-C pieces.

2: Glue cabochons to right sides as indicated on graphs.

3: For antennae (make 3 pair), place eight same color seed beads on each pearl head pin. Stick victorian gold bead assemblies into Small Butterfly (see photo), copper bead assemblies in Medium Butterfly and Silver bead assemblies in Large Butterfly. Glue each antennae to secure.

4: Hang or display as desired.

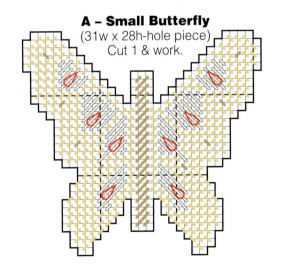

A – Small Butterfly
(31w x 28h-hole piece)
Cut 1 & work.

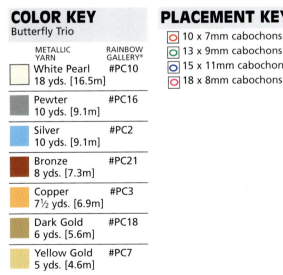

COLOR KEY
Butterfly Trio

METALLIC YARN		RAINBOW GALLERY®
White Pearl 18 yds. [16.5m]		#PC10
Pewter 10 yds. [9.1m]		#PC16
Silver 10 yds. [9.1m]		#PC2
Bronze 8 yds. [7.3m]		#PC21
Copper 7½ yds. [6.9m]		#PC3
Dark Gold 6 yds. [5.6m]		#PC18
Yellow Gold 5 yds. [4.6m]		#PC7

PLACEMENT KEY

⬭	10 x 7mm cabochons
⬭	13 x 9mm cabochons
⬭	15 x 11mm cabochons
⬭	18 x 8mm cabochons

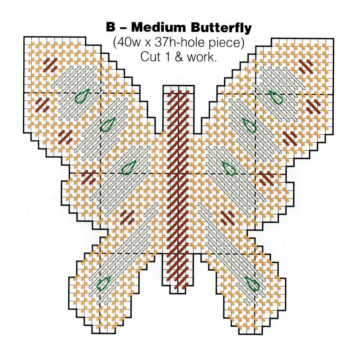

B – Medium Butterfly
(40w x 37h-hole piece)
Cut 1 & work.

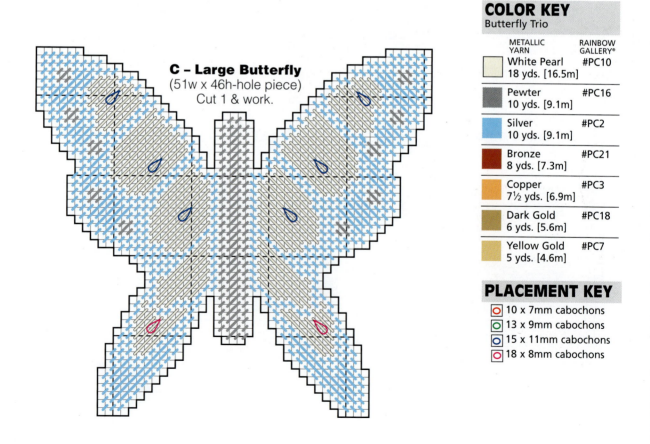

C – Large Butterfly
(51w x 46h-hole piece)
Cut 1 & work.

COLOR KEY
Butterfly Trio

	METALLIC YARN	RAINBOW GALLERY®
	White Pearl 18 yds. [16.5m]	#PC10
	Pewter 10 yds. [9.1m]	#PC16
	Silver 10 yds. [9.1m]	#PC2
	Bronze 8 yds. [7.3m]	#PC21
	Copper 7½ yds. [6.9m]	#PC3
	Dark Gold 6 yds. [5.6m]	#PC18
	Yellow Gold 5 yds. [4.6m]	#PC7

PLACEMENT KEY

- 10 x 7mm cabochons
- 13 x 9mm cabochons
- 15 x 11mm cabochons
- 18 x 8mm cabochons

Candle Holder Set

Designed by Joan Green

Use plastic canvas shapes to create these stylish multi-purpose holders.

SIZES
Heart is 6½" across x 1½" [16.5cm x 3.8cm];
Star is 5½" across x 1½" tall [14cm x 3.8cm].

MATERIALS
• One sheet of 7-mesh plastic canvas
• Two plastic canvas heart shapes
• Two plastic canvas star shapes
• One 9" x 12" [22.9cm x 30.5cm] sheet of white felt
• Two 2" [5.1cm] diameter candles; Ten 5mm pearl beads
• Sewing needle and white thread
• Small amount of potpourri
• Artificial greenery
• Metallic yarn (for amounts see Color Key)
• Worsted-weight or plastic canvas yarn (for amounts see Color Key).

CUTTING INSTRUCTIONS
   A: For Heart Box Top, cut one from heart shape according to graph.
   B: For Heart Box Sides, cut two 65w x 9h-holes.
   C: For Heart Box Bottom, use one heart shape (no graph).
   D: For Star Box Top, cut one from star shape according to graph.
   E: For Star Box Sides, cut ten 11w x 9h-holes.

F: For Star Box Bottom, use one star shape (no graph).

STITCHING INSTRUCTIONS
NOTE: C and F pieces are not worked.

1: Using colors and stitches indicated, work A, B, D and E pieces according to graphs; with eggshell, overcast cutout edges of A and D pieces.

2: Using sewing needle and thread, sew pearls to E pieces as indicated on graphs.

NOTE: For linings, using C and F pieces as patterns, cut one each from felt ⅛" [3mm] smaller at all edges

3: With eggshell, whipstitch A-C pieces together according to Heart Holder Assembly Illustration and D-F pieces together according to Star Holder Assembly Illustration.

4: Glue corresponding linings to bottom of each assembly; place candles inside each assembly, placing greenery and potpourri around each candle (see photo).

B – Heart Box Side
(65w x 9h-hole pieces) Cut 2 & work.

Star Holder Assembly Illustration
(Pieces are shown in different colors for contrast; gray denotes wrong side.)

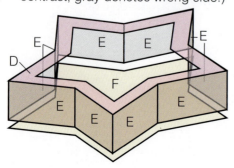

Spider Web Rose Stitch Illustration

Work five spokes into the same central hole. Weave yarn over & under spokes, keeping tension slightly loose. Continue weaving until spokes are fully covered. Pull yarn slightly to "puff" rose.

A – Heart Box Top
(Use 1 heart shape)
Cut out gray area & work.

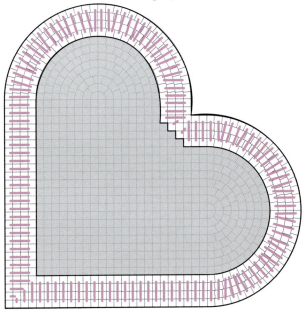

Heart Holder
Assembly Illustration
(Pieces are shown in different colors for
contrast; gray denotes wrong side.)

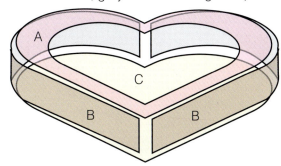

E – Star Box Side
(11w x 9h-hole pieces)
Cut 10 & work.

COLOR KEY
Candle Holder Set

	METALLIC YARN	RAINBOW GALLERY®
Pink 16 yds. [14.6m]		#PC8
Copper 8 yds. [7.3m]		#PC3
Forest Green 8 yds. [7.3m]		#PC17
Purple 3 yds. [2.7m]		#PC15
	WORSTED-WEIGHT	RED HEART CLASSIC®
Eggshell 26 yds. [23.8m]		#111

OTHER KEY
Spider Web Rose
Pearl Placement

D – Star Box Top
(Use 1 star shape)
Cut out gray area & work.

Grandma's Garden Frame

Designed by Janna Britton

Make it easy for grandma to display her most beautiful blossoms with this flower frame.

SIZE
8¾" [22.2cm] across.

MATERIALS
- ½ sheet of 7-mesh plastic canvas
- One 3" [7.6cm] plastic canvas circle
- One 4" [10.2cm] plastic canvas circle
- 2 yds. [1.8m] of yellow baby rickrack
- 2½" [6.4cm] circle of yellow cardstock or photo of choice
- Six 1½" x 2" [3.8cm x 5.1cm] photos of choice
- Sewing needle and yellow thread
- Worsted-weight or plastic canvas yarn (for amounts see Color Key).

CUTTING INSTRUCTIONS
A: For Petals, cut six according to graph.

B: For Flower Backing, cut away three outer rows of holes from 4" circle (no graph).

C: For Flower Center, cut 3" circle according to graph.

STITCHING INSTRUCTIONS
NOTE: B is not worked.

1: Using colors and stitches indicated, work A and C pieces according to graphs; with watermelon for Petals and yellow for Flower Center, overcast edges of A and C pieces.

NOTE: Cut six 6½" [16.5cm] lengths of rickrack.

2: With needle and thread, tack one length of rickrack to each Petal as indicated on graph. (Tack where indicated so that photo corners may be inserted under rickrack.)

3: With watermelon, overlapping pieces two holes, tack Petals to B according to Frame Assembly Illustration.

4: Glue yellow cardstock circle or photo to B; glue wrong side of C to right side of Frame assembly over circle cardstock or photo. Insert photos around each Petal as shown.

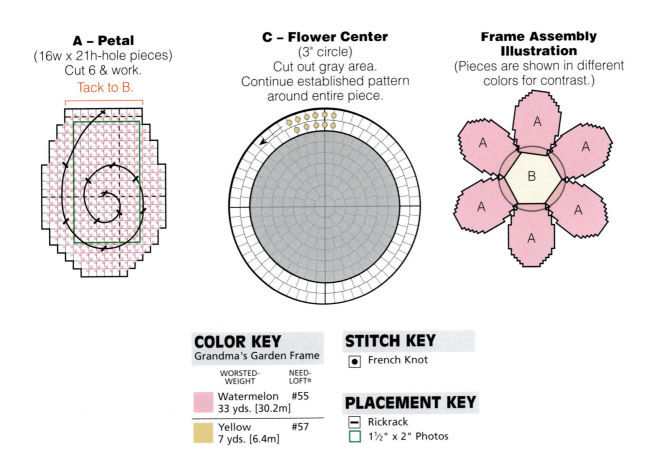

A – Petal
(16w x 21h-hole pieces)
Cut 6 & work.
Tack to B.

C – Flower Center
(3" circle)
Cut out gray area.
Continue established pattern
around entire piece.

**Frame Assembly
Illustration**
(Pieces are shown in different
colors for contrast.)

COLOR KEY
Grandma's Garden Frame

	WORSTED-WEIGHT	NEED-LOFT®
Watermelon	#55	
33 yds. [30.2m]		
Yellow	#57	
7 yds. [6.4m]		

STITCH KEY
- ⊙ French Knot

PLACEMENT KEY
- ⊟ Rickrack
- ☐ 1½" x 2" Photos

Happy Holly Days

Designed by Angie Arickx

Express your sentiments with this colorful seasonal sign.

SIZE
5½" x 10⅞" [14cm x 27.6cm].

MATERIALS
• One sheet of 7-mesh plastic canvas
• Worsted-weight or plastic canvas yarn
  (for amounts see Color Key).

CUTTING INSTRUCTIONS
For Holly Days, cut one 72w x 36h-holes.

STITCHING INSTRUCTIONS
1: Using colors and stitches indicated, work piece according to graph.

2: With white, overcast edges. Hang as desired.

COLOR KEY
Happy Holly Days

	WORSTED-WEIGHT	NEED-LOFT®
☐	White 28 yds. [25.6m]	#41
	Christmas Green 10 yds. [9.1m]	#28
	Christmas Red 6 yds. [5.5m]	#02
	Burgundy 3 yds. [2.7m]	#03
	Forest 2 yds. [1.8m]	#29

Holly Days
(72w x 36h-hole piece) Cut 1 & work, filling in uncoded area using white & continental stitch.

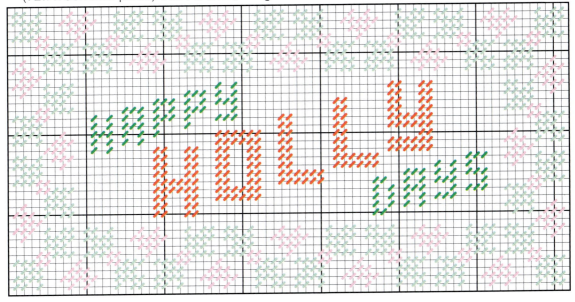

Life Began In A Garden

Designed by Ruby Thacker

This heartwarming message will make family and friends feel right at home.

SIZE

4½" x 7½" [11.4cm x 19cm], not including hanger or embellishments.

MATERIALS

- ¼ sheet of 10-mesh plastic canvas
- ⅓ sheet of 7-mesh plastic canvas
- 16" [40.6cm] length of ¼" [6mm] green twisted cord
- Two 1½" [3.8cm] green tassels
- Sewing needle and green thread
- Craft glue or glue gun
- Six-strand embroidery floss (for amounts see Color Key)
- Worsted-weight or plastic canvas yarn (for amounts see Color Key).

CUTTING INSTRUCTIONS

NOTE: Cut A and G pieces from 7-mesh and remaining pieces from 10-mesh canvas.

A: For Sign, cut one 49w x 30h-holes.
B: For Rose Outer Petals, cut two according to graph.
C: For Rose Inner Petals, cut two according to graph.
D: For Medium Flowers, cut six according to graph.
E: For Small Flowers, cut fifteen according to graph.
F: For Leaves, cut six according to graph.
G: For Holder Piece, cut two 5w x 4h-holes.

STITCHING INSTRUCTIONS

1: Using colors and stitches indicated, work A-G pieces according to graphs. Omitting attachement areas, with forest for Sign, med. lavender for Small Flowers and with matching colors, overcast A-G pieces.

2: Using floss in colors and embroidery stitches indicated, embroider detail on A and C-E pieces as indicated on graphs.

3: For Medium Flower Buds, with peach, tack opposite corners together on two D pieces (See Flower Bud Assembly Illustration on page 108.)

4: For Holders, with forest, whipstitch ends of each G piece to A as indicated. Thread ends of cord through Holder Pieces (see photo); using needle and thread, sew tassels to ends of cord.

5: For Roses (make 2), glue one Rose Inner Petal inside each Rose Outer Petal

6: Glue Roses, Medium Flowers, Small Flowers, Flower Buds and leaves to Sign as shown in photo.

COLOR KEY
Life Began In A Garden

12-STRAND EMBROIDERY FLOSS		DMC®
■	Lt. Green 7 yds. [6..4m]	#701
□	Med. Lavender 3 yds. [2.7m]	#210

6-STRAND EMBROIDERY FLOSS		DMC®
■	Lt. Cyclamen Pink 11 yds. [10.1m]	#3806
■	Peach 3 yds. [2.7m]	#353
■	Vy. Lt. Topaz 2 yds. [1.8m]	#727

WORSTED-WEIGHT		NEED-LOFT®
□	White 22 yds. [20.1m]	#41
■	Black 3 yds. [2.7m]	#00
■	Forest 3 yds. [2.7m]	#29

STITCH KEY

- — Backstitch/Straight
- • French Knot

A – Sign
(49w x 30h-hole piece) Cut 1 from 7-mesh & work, filling in uncoded area using white & continental stitch.

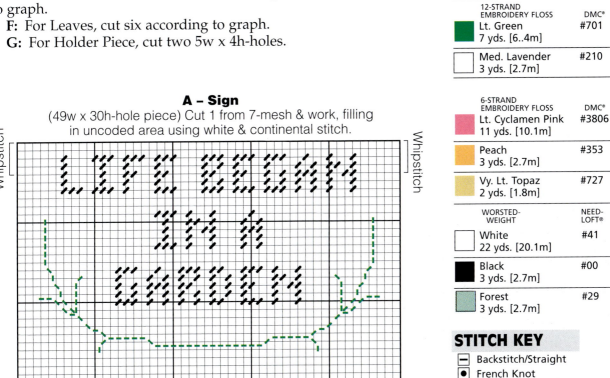

B – Rose Outer Petal
(13w x 13h-hole pieces)
Cut 2 from 10-mesh & work

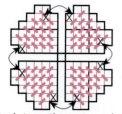

Tack together at each X,
overlapping Petals.

C – Rose Inner Petal
(11w x 11h-hole pieces)
Cut 2 from 10-mesh & work.

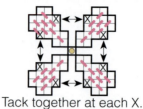

Tack together at each X.

D – Medium Flower
(5w x 5h-hole pieces)
Cut 6 from 10-mesh & work.

E – Small Flower
(3w x 3h-hole pieces)
Cut 15 from 10-mesh.

F – Leaf
(6w x 6h-hole pieces)
Cut 6 from 10-mesh & work.

G – Holder Piece
(5w x 4h-hole pieces)
Cut 2 from 7-mesh & work.

Whipstitch   Whipstitch

COLOR KEY
Life Began In A Garden

	12-STRAND EMBROIDERY FLOSS	DMC®
■	Lt. Green 7 yds. [6..4m]	#701
□	Med. Lavender 3 yds. [2.7m]	#210

	6-STRAND EMBROIDERY FLOSS	DMC®
■	Lt. Cyclamen Pink 11 yds. [10.1m]	#3806
■	Peach 3 yds. [2.7m]	#353
■	Vy. Lt. Topaz 2 yds. [1.8m]	#727

	WORSTED-WEIGHT	NEED-LOFT®
□	White 22 yds. [20.1m]	#41
■	Black 3 yds. [2.7m]	#00
■	Forest 3 yds. [2.7m]	#29

Flower Bud Assembly Illustration

D —

STITCH KEY
⊟	Backstitch/Straight
⊡	French Knot

Flower Pot Angels

Designed by Ruby Thacker

These unique miniature angels will look great on your tree or mantel.

SIZE
About 1¾" across x 2⅜" [4.4cm x 6cm], not including hanger.

MATERIALS FOR ONE
- Scrap piece of 10-mesh plastic canvas
- One mini terra-cotta pot
- One 25mm smiling wooden doll head
- Curly crepe wool doll hair
- One 12mm gold liberty bell
- One 6mm gold jewelry jump ring
- Acrylic paint in color of choice
- Craft glue or glue gun
- Metallic floss (for amount see Color Key)
- Six-strand embroidery floss (for amounts see Color Key).

CUTTING INSTRUCTIONS
A: For Arms, cut one according to graph.
B: For Wings, cut two according to graph.
C: For Halo, cut one 31w x 1h-hole (no graph).

STITCHING INSTRUCTIONS
NOTE: Use 12 strands floss for entire project.

1: Using colors and stitches indicated, work A and B pieces according to graphs. With gold for Halo (overlap ends three holes to join) and with matching colors, overcast edges of A-C.

2: With gold and backstitch, embroider detail on Wings as indicated on graph.

NOTE: Paint pot; let dry.

3: Using jump ring, attach liberty bell to Arms (see photo); glue arms to pot. Glue hair to doll head and head to pot. Glue Halo to top of head and wrong side of Wings to back of Angel (see photo). Style angel hair as desired.

4: Hang or display as desired.

A – Arms
(21w x 8h-hole piece)
Cut 1 & work.

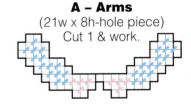

B – Wings
(16w x 11h-hole pieces)
Cut 2 & work together as one.

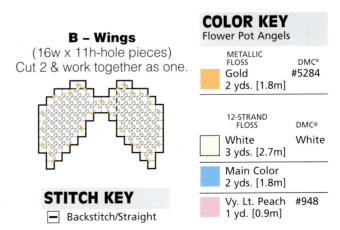

STITCH KEY
- ▭ Backstitch/Straight

COLOR KEY
Flower Pot Angels

METALLIC FLOSS		DMC®
🟧	Gold 2 yds. [1.8m]	#5284

12-STRAND FLOSS		DMC®
⬜	White 3 yds. [2.7m]	White
🟦	Main Color 2 yds. [1.8m]	
🟪	Vy. Lt. Peach 1 yd. [0.9m]	#948

Tulip Accessories

Designed by Kristine Loffredo

Wear a touch of spring with these pastel florals.

SIZE
Each Tulip is 1⅛" x 1¼" [2.9cm x 3.2cm].

MATERIALS
- ½ sheet of 7-mesh plastic canvas
- Six metal button covers
- 1½" [3.8cm] silver bar pin
- One 3" [7.6cm] barrette clip
- Craft glue or glue gun
- #32 Braid thread (for amounts see Color Key)

CUTTING INSTRUCTIONS
For Tulips, cut twelve according to graph.

STITCHING INSTRUCTIONS
1: Using colors and stitches indicated, work pieces according to graph; with matching colors, overcast edges.

2: Glue one of each color Tulip to pin and to barrette (see photo). Glue one each of remaining Tulips to button covers.

Tulip
(7w x 7h-hole pieces)
Cut 12. Work 4;
substituting star pink &
star yellow for periwinkle,
work 4 in each color.

COLOR KEY
Tulip Accessories

#32 BRAID THREAD	- KREINIK
Periwinkle 4 yds. [3.7m]	#9294
Star Pink 4 yds. [3.7m]	#092
Star Yellow 4 yds. [3.7m]	#091

Puppy Night Light

Designed by Debbie Tabor

This guard dog is sure to keep watch all through the night.

SIZE
1½" x 7½" x 8½" tall [3.8cm x 19cm x 21.6cm].

MATERIALS
- One sheet of 7-mesh plastic canvas
- One model GNII night light
- Craft glue or glue gun
- Six-strand embroidery floss (for amounts see Color Key)
- Worsted-weight or plastic canvas yarn (for amounts see Color Key).

CUTTING INSTRUCTIONS
A: For Body, cut one according to graph.

B: For Paws #1 and #2, cut one each according to graphs.

C: For Lantern Top Side Pieces #1 and #2, cut one each according to graphs.

D: For Lantern Top Front Piece, cut one according to graph.

E: For Lantern Front, cut one according to graph.

F: For Lantern Sides, cut two according to graph.

G: For Lantern Handle, cut one 18w x 1h-hole (no graph).

STITCHING INSTRUCTIONS
1: Using colors and stitches indicated, work A-D pieces according to graphs; omitting attachment areas, with matching colors, overcast edges of A and B pieces. With black for cutouts on Lantern Front and Lantern Sides and edges of Lantern Handle, overcast E-G pieces.

2: Using yarn and floss in colors and embroidery stitches indicated, embroider detail on A and B pieces as indicated on graphs.

3: With matching colors, whipstitch A-G pieces together according to Night Light Assembly Illustration.

4: Insert night light through cutout on wrong side of Body; glue to secure.

C – Lantern Top Side Piece #1 & #2
(7w x 7h-hole pieces)
Cut 1 each & work.

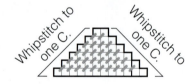

D – Lantern Top Front Piece
(12w x 6h-hole piece)
Cut 1 & work.

E – Lantern Front
(12w x 23h-hole piece)
Cut 1.

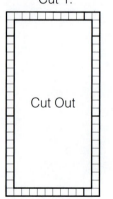

Cut Out

F – Lantern Side
(7w x 23h-hole pieces)
Cut 2.

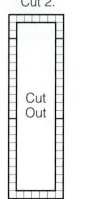

Cut Out

Night Light Assembly Illustration
(Pieces are shown in different colors for contrast; gray denotes wrong side.)

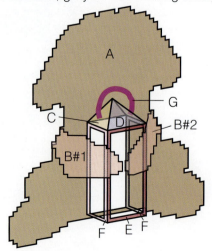

A – Body
(50w x 55h-hole piece) Cut 1 & work.

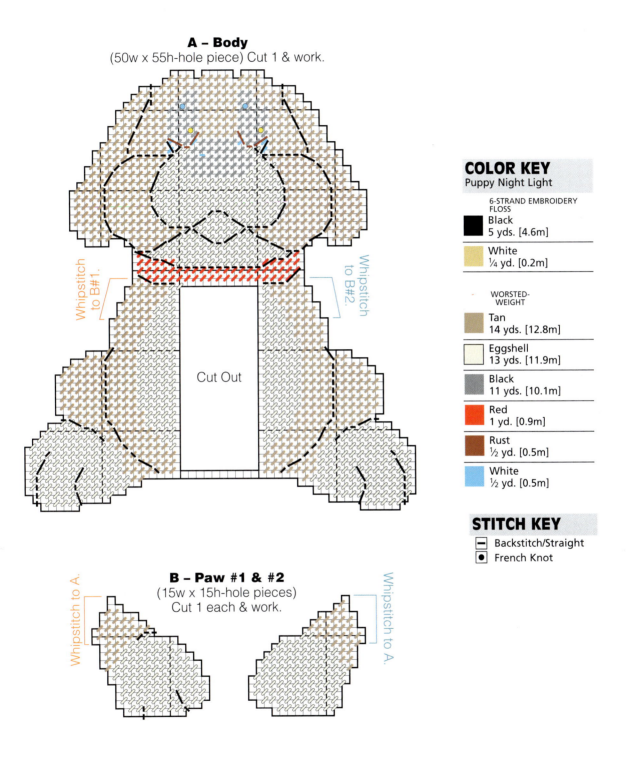

Whipstitch to B#1.

Whipstitch to B#2.

Cut Out

B – Paw #1 & #2
(15w x 15h-hole pieces)
Cut 1 each & work.

Whipstitch to A.

Whipstitch to A.

Happy Veggies

Designed by Janelle Giese

*"Don't forget to eat your vegetables" is one of many reminders
these happy fridgie magnets can display.*

SIZES

Corn is 3½" x 5" [8.9cm x 12.7cm];
Tomato is 3⅛" x 3⅜" [7.9cm x 8.6cm];
Carrot is 3¼" x 5⅜" [8.3cm x 13.7cm].

MATERIALS

- ½ sheet of 7-mesh plastic canvas
- Three 1" [2.5cm] button magnets
- Craft glue or glue gun
- No. 3 pearl cotton (coton perlé) (for amount see Color Key)
- No. 5 pearl cotton (coton perlé) (for amount see Color Key)
- Worsted-weight or plastic canvas yarn (for amounts see Color Key).

CUTTING INSTRUCTIONS

A: For Corn, cut one according to graph.
B: For Tomato, cut one according to graph.
C: For Carrot, cut one according to graph.

STITCHING INSTRUCTIONS

1: Using colors indicated and continental stitch, work pieces according to graphs; with matching colors as shown in photo, overcast edges.

2: Using pearl cotton and yarn in colors and embroidery stitches indicated, embroider detail on pieces as indicated on graphs.

3: Glue one magnet to wrong side of each piece. Display as desired.

C – Carrot
(21w x 35h-hole piece)
Cut 1 & work.

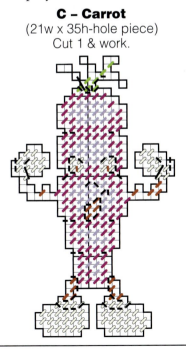

A – Corn
(22w x 33h-hole piece)
Cut 1 & work.

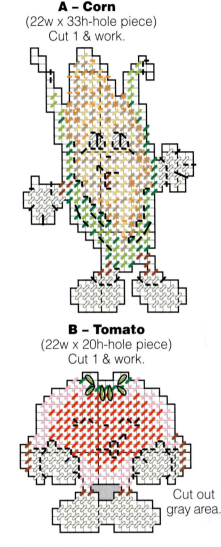

B – Tomato
(22w x 20h-hole piece)
Cut 1 & work.

Cut out gray area.

COLOR KEY
Happy Veggies

NO. 3 PEARL COTTON	DMC®
Med. Topaz 2 yds. [1.8m]	#783

NO. 5 PEARL COTTON	DMC®
Black 6 yds. [5.5m]	#310

WORSTED-WEIGHT	NEED-LOFT®
White 7 yds. [6.4m]	#41
Christmas Green 3 yds. [2.7m]	#28
Pumpkin 3 yds. [2.7m]	#12
Mermaid 8 yds. [7.3m]	#53
Sail Blue 8 yds. [7.3m]	#35

WORSTED-WEIGHT	NEED-LOFT®
Black 2 yds. [1.8m]	#00
Christmas Red 2 yds. [1.8m]	#02
Fern 2 yds. [1.8m]	#23
Lemon 2 yds. [1.8m]	#20
Red 2 yds. [1.8m]	#01
Tangerine 2 yds. [1.8m]	#11
Yellow 2 yds. [1.8m]	#57

STITCH KEY

- ⊟ Backstitch/Straight
- ⬭ Lazy Daisy

Pansy Motif Basket

Designed by Janelle Giese

Turn the ordinary into the spectacular with this simple yet beautiful pansy motif.

SIZE
Motif is 3½" x 5" [8.9cm x 12.7cm].

MATERIALS
• ¼ sheet of 7-mesh plastic canvas
• One basket of choice; 18" [45.7cm] length of twisted craft paper in color of choice 18" [45.7cm] length of raffia straw
• Craft glue or glue gun
• No. 3 pearl cotton (coton perlé) (for amounts see Color Key)
• Worsted-weight or plastic canvas yarn (for amounts see Color Key).

CUTTING INSTRUCTIONS
For Pansy Motif, cut one according to graph.

STITCHING INSTRUCTIONS
1: Using colors and stitches indicated, work piece according to graph; with dk. plum for flowers and forest green for leaves, overcast edges of piece.

2: Using pearl cotton and yarn in colors and embroidery stitches indicated, embroider detail on piece as indicated on graph.

3: Untwist craft paper; shape craft paper and raffia into a bow (see photo). Glue craft paper and raffia to basket; glue Pansy Motif to center of bow.

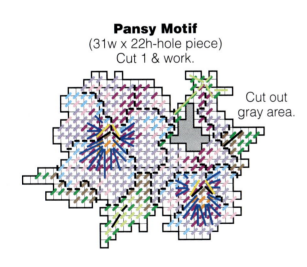

Pansy Motif
(31w x 22h-hole piece)
Cut 1 & work.

Cut out gray area.

COLOR KEY
Pansy Motif Basket

NO. 3 PEARL COTTON		DMC®
■	Black 3 yds. [2.7m]	#310
■	Dk. Navy Blue 2 yds. [1.8m]	#823

WORSTED-WEIGHT		RED HEART® CLASSSIC™
■	Dk. Plum 3 yds. [2.7m]	#533
■	Forest Green 2 yds. [1.8m]	#689
■	Lt. Plum 2 yds. [1.8m]	#531
■	Black 1 yd. [0.9m]	#12
■	Cameo Rose 1 yd. [0.9m]	#759
■	Country Blue 1 yd. [0.9m]	#531
■	Orange 1 yd. [0.9m]	#245
■	Paddy Green 1 yd. [0.9m]	#686
■	White 1 yd. [0.9m]	#1

STITCH KEY
⊟ Backstitch/Straight

"Frosty" Can Cozy

Designed by Susan Leinberger

This "cool" can cozy will make a great party favor.

SIZE
4" across x 4½" tall [10.2cm x 11.4cm].

MATERIALS
- ½ sheet of 7-mesh plastic canvas
- One 3" [7.6cm] plastic canvas circle
- One 4" [10.2cm] plastic canvas circle
- 10" [25.4cm] length of 5⁄8" [16mm] ribbon of choice
- Two 3⁄8" [10mm] red jingle bells
- Three 7⁄8" [2.2cm] green leaf sequins
- Craft glue or glue gun
- Metallic craft cord (for amounts see Color Key)
- Worsted-weight or plastic canvas yarn (for amounts see Color Key).

CUTTING INSTRUCTIONS
A: For Side, cut one 67w x 28h-holes.
B: For Nose, cut two according to graph.
C: For Hat Brim, cut one from 4" circle according to graph.
D: For Bottom, use one 3" circle (no graph).

STITCHING INSTRUCTIONS
NOTE: D is not worked.

1: Using colors and stitches indicated, work A-C pieces according to graphs (see Ribbed Wheel Stitch Diagram); with matching colors, overcast top edges of A and edges of C piece.

2: With black and smyrna cross, embroider eyes on A as indicated on graph.

3: With bittersweet, holding B pieces wrong sides together, whipstitch together, forming Nose. Whipstitch Nose to A as indicated.

4: With red cord, whipstitch D to A; place Hat Brim over A as shown in photo and glue to secure.

5: Glue ribbon around A above Hat Brim; glue leaf sequins and jingle bells to top of Hat Brim as shown.

C – Hat Brim
(4" circle) Cut 1 & work.
Cut away gray area.

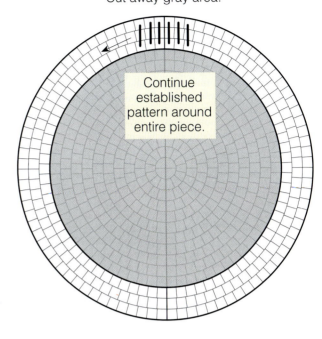

Continue established pattern around entire piece.

COLOR KEY
Frosty Can Cozy

	METALLIC CRAFT CORD	NEED-LOFT®
Red 6 yds. [5.5m]		#03
Green 4 yds. [3.7m]		#04

	WORSTED-WEIGHT	NEED-LOFT®
White 16 yds. [14.6m]		#41
Black 12 yds. [11m]		#00
Bittersweet 2 yds. [1.8m]		#52
Watermelon 2 yds. [1.8m]		#55

B – Nose Piece
(8w x 3h-hole pieces)
Cut 2. Work 1 & 1 reversed.

OTHER KEY
✱ Smyrna Cross
◯ Ribbed Wheel
☐ Nose/Side Attachment

Ribbed Wheel Stitch Diagram
(Yarn is shown in different colors for clarity.)

Step 1: Stitch an 8-spoke wheel with a central hole.

Step 2: Bring needle up near central hole.

Step 3: Working in a circular pattern from center outward, wrap yarn around each spoke on each round until spokes are completely covered.

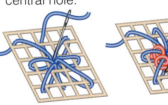

A – Side
(67w x 28h-hole piece) Cut 1 & work, overlapping ends three holes & working through both thicknesses at overlap area to join.

Lap Over

Lap Under

Butterfly Motif Basket

Designed by Janelle Giese

Add a touch of nature to your next project with this life-like monarch.

SIZE
Motif is 5¼" x 6" [13.3cm x 15.2cm].

MATERIALS
- ½ sheet of 7-mesh plastic canvas
- One basket of choice
- Two 18" [45.7cm] lengths of ivory twisted craft paper
- One 18" [45.7cm] length of dk. red and tan twisted craft paper
- Three 18" [45.7cm] lengths of raffia straw
- Craft glue or glue gun
- No. 3 pearl cotton (coton perlé) (for amounts see Color Key)
- No. 5 pearl cotton (coton perlé) (for amount see Color Key)
- Worsted-weight or plastic canvas yarn (for amounts see Color Key).

CUTTING INSTRUCTIONS
For Butterfly Motif, cut one according to graph.

STITCHING INSTRUCTIONS
1: Using colors and stitches indicated, work piece according to graph; with matching colors as shown in photo, overcast edges of piece.

2: Using pearl cotton in colors and embroidery stitches indicated, embroider detail on piece as indicated on graph.

NOTE: Cut one 2½" [6.4cm] and one 1" [2.5cm] length of No. 5 pearl cotton.

3: For large Butterfly antennae, using 2½" length, from back to front, insert each end through one hole as indicated, glue to secure. For small Butterfly antennae, glue 1" length of pearl cotton to wrong side of Motif at hole as shown in photo. Glue to secure.

4: Untwist craft paper, shape ivory craft paper into two loops; shape dk. red and tan craft paper into a bow. Glue loops on top of Bow. Tie each raffia length into a bow and glue to top of craft paper assembly (see photo). Glue Butterfly to center of craft paper assembly and assembly to basket.

Butterfly Motif
(36w x 31h-hole piece) Cut 1 & work.

Cut out gray area.

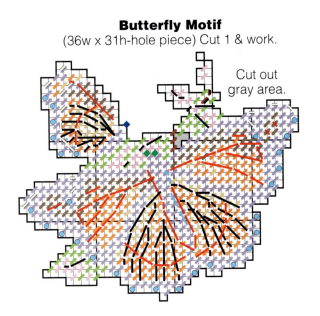

COLOR KEY
Butterfly Motif Basket

NO. 3 PEARL COTTON	DMC®
■ Black	#310
2 yds. [1.8m]	
■ White	
2 yds. [1.8m]	

NO. 5 PEARL COTTON	DMC®
■ Black	#310
4 yds. [3.7m]	

WORSTED-WEIGHT	NEED-LOFT®
■ Black	#00
6 yds. [5.5m]	
■ Pumpkin	#12
4 yds. [3.7m]	

WORSTED-WEIGHT	NEED-LOFT®
■ Moss	#25
2 yds. [1.8m]	
■ Rust	#09
2 yds. [1.8m]	
■ Tangerine	#11
2 yds. [1.8m]	
■ Camel	#43
1 yd. [0.9m]	
■ Silver	#37
1 yd. [0.9m]	
□ White	#41
1 yd. [1.9m]	

STITCH KEY
- ─ Backstitch/Straight
- ● French Knot

Baby Blossoms

Designed by Mary T. Cosgrove

Precious moments can be displayed in this dainty flower frame.

SIZE
1½" x 4" x 4" tall [3.8cm x 10.2cm x 10.2cm].

MATERIALS
• ½ sheet of 7-mesh plastic canvas
• 9" [22.9cm] length of yellow ¼" [6mm] satin ribbon
• Craft glue or glue gun
• Worsted-weight or plastic canvas yarn (for amounts see Color Key).

CUTTING INSTRUCTIONS
A: For Front, cut one according to graph.
B: For Flowers, cut two according to graph.
C: For Back, cut one 26w x 25h-holes (no graph).
D: For Long Stand Piece, cut one 11w x 25h-holes (no graph).
E: For Short Stand Piece, cut one 11w x 8h-holes. (no graph).

STITCHING INSTRUCTIONS
NOTE: C-E pieces are not worked.

1: Using colors and stitches indicated, work A and B pieces according to graphs; with lemon for cutout on A and with matching colors, overcast indicated areas of A and B pieces.

2: Using lemon and French knot, embroider centers on B pieces as indicated on graph.

3: With lemon, whipstitch A and C-E pieces together according to Frame Assembly Diagram; overcast unfinished top edges of Frame.

4: Tie ribbon into a bow; glue bow and Flowers to Frame as shown in photo.

B – Flower
(5w x 5h-hole pieces)
Cut 2. Work 1; substituting pink for sail blue, work 1.

A – Front
(26w x 25h-hole piece) Cut 1 & work, filling in uncoded area using white & continental stitch.

Whipstitch to E between arrows.

COLOR KEY
Baby Blossoms

	WORSTED-WEIGHT	NEED-LOFT®
Lemon	5 yds. [4.6m]	#20
White	4 yds. [3.7m]	#41
Pink	2 yds. [1.8m]	#07
Sail Blue	2 yds. [1.8m]	#35

STITCH KEY
● French Knot

Frame Assembly Diagram
(Pieces are shown in different colors for contrast.)

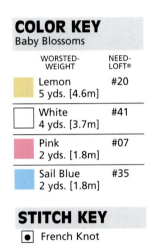

Step 1: Whipstitch one short end of D & E pieces together.

Step 2: Whipstitch C to wrong side of A, working in edge of E as you work.

Step 3: Overcast unfinished edges of A & C; work in edge of D as you overcast C.

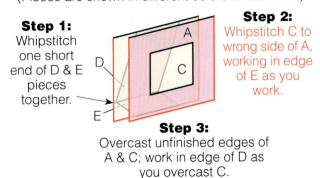

You Are My Sunshine

Designed by Mary T. Cosgrove

Show off each ray of sunshine in your life in this adorable frame.

SIZE
10½" x 10½" [26.7cm x 26.7cm].

MATERIALS
- One sheet of 7-mesh plastic canvas
- 12"-square [30.5cm] sheet of posterboard or cardboard
- Eight 2"-square [5.2cm] photos of choice
- Craft glue or glue gun
- Metallic cord (for amount see Color Key)
- Worsted-weight or plastic canvas yarn (for amounts see Color Key).

CUTTING INSTRUCTIONS
For Frame, cut one according to graph.

STITCHING INSTRUCTIONS
1: Using colors and stitches indicated, work piece according to graph.

2: Using cord and yarn in colors and embroidery stitches indicated, embroider detail on piece as indicated on graph.

NOTE: *For backing, using piece as a pattern, omitting cutouts, cut one from posterboard or cardboard ⅛" [3mm] smaller at all edges.*

3: Glue one photo to wrong side over each cutout; glue backing to wrong side of piece.

4: Hang or display as desired.

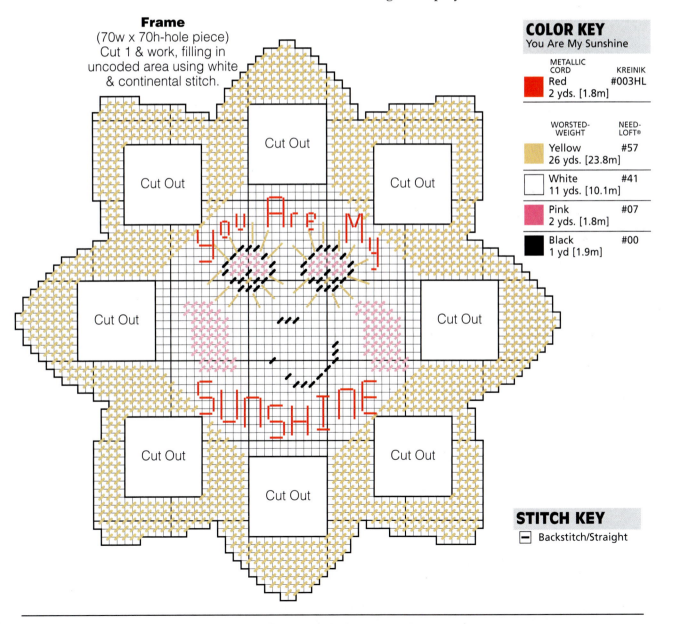

Frame
(70w x 70h-hole piece)
Cut 1 & work, filling in uncoded area using white & continental stitch.

COLOR KEY
You Are My Sunshine

	METALLIC CORD	KREINIK
Red	2 yds. [1.8m]	#003HL

	WORSTED-WEIGHT	NEED-LOFT®
Yellow	26 yds. [23.8m]	#57
White	11 yds. [10.1m]	#41
Pink	2 yds. [1.8m]	#07
Black	1 yd [1.9m]	#00

STITCH KEY
- Backstitch/Straight

Christmas Bow

Designed by Mary T. Cosgrove

Favorite holiday moments will never be forgotten
when displayed in this cute bow frame.

SIZE
8" x 10" [20.3cm x 25.4cm] with a 4¼" x 5" [10.8cm x 12.7cm] photo window.

MATERIALS
- One sheet of 7-mesh plastic canvas
- One photo of choice
- Worsted-weight or plastic canvas yarn (for amounts see Color Key).

CUTTING INSTRUCTIONS
A: For Front, cut one according to graph.
B: For Back, cut one according to graph.

STITCHING INSTRUCTIONS
NOTE: B is not worked.

1: Using colors and stitches indicated, work A according to graph; with white, overcast large cutout on A.

2: Holding Back to wrong side of Front, with white, whipstitch outer edges and small cutout together; overcast unfinished edges of Front.

3: Insert photo between Front and Back; display as desired.

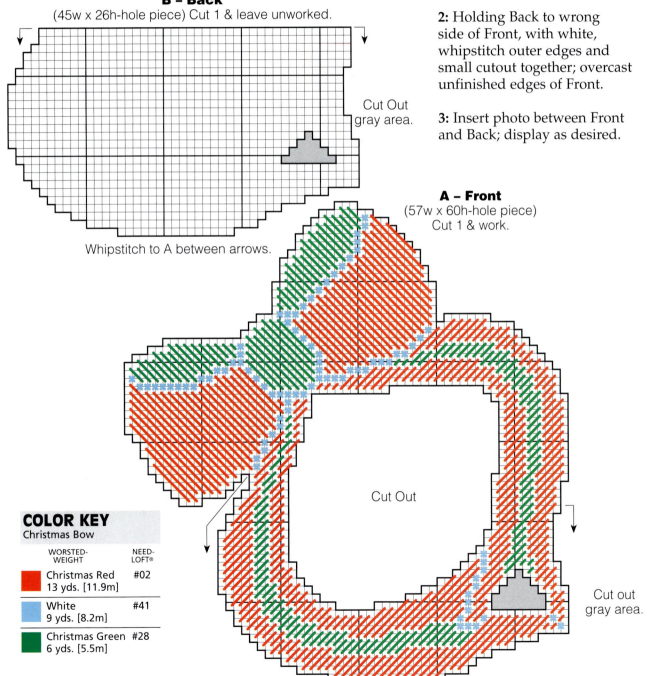

B – Back
(45w x 26h-hole piece) Cut 1 & leave unworked.

Cut Out gray area.

Whipstitch to A between arrows.

A – Front
(57w x 60h-hole piece)
Cut 1 & work.

Cut Out

Cut out gray area.

COLOR KEY
Christmas Bow

	WORSTED-WEIGHT	NEED-LOFT®
■ Christmas Red 13 yds. [11.9m]		#02
■ White 9 yds. [8.2m]		#41
■ Christmas Green 6 yds. [5.5m]		#28

Whipstitch to B between arrows.

Heart Frames

Designed by Darla Fanton

Decorate your teenager's room with pictures of her special friends in these friendship frames!

SIZES

Wired Heart Frame and Open Heart Frame are each 2½" x 5¾" x 5¼" tall [6.4cm x 14.6m x 13.3cm], not including embellishments. Wired Heart Frame has a 4" x 4½" [10.2cm x 11.4cm] photo window and Open Heart Frame has a 3½" x 3¾" [8.9cm x 9.5cm] photo window; Heart Shaped Frame is 2½" x 7" x 5⅜" tall [6.4cm x 17.8cm x 13.7cm] with a 3¾" x 4¾" [9.5cm x 12.1cm] photo window.

MATERIALS

- Three sheets of 7-mesh plastic canvas
- 2 yds. of 22-gauge copper wire
- Assorted color and sizes of beads
- Three photos of choice
- Craft glue or glue gun
- ⅛" metallic ribbon (for amounts see individual Color Keys)
- Worsted-weight or plastic canvas yarn (for amounts see individual Color Keys).

CUTTING INSTRUCTIONS

A: For Wired Heart Frame Front, cut one according to graph.
B: For Wired Heart Frame Heart #1, cut one according to graph.
C: For Wired Heart Frame Heart #2, cut one according to graph.
D: For Wired Heart Frame Heart #3, cut one according to graph.
E: For Wired Heart Frame and Open Heart Frame Backs, cut one each 38w x 33h-holes.
F: For Stand Pieces, cut twelve according to graph.
G: For Open Heart Frame Front, cut one according to graph.

H: For Heart Shaped Frame Front, cut one according to graph.
I: For Heart Shaped Frame Back, cut one according to graph.

STITCHING INSTRUCTIONS

NOTE: E, F and I piece are not worked.

1: Using colors and stitches indicated, work A-D, G and H pieces according to graphs; with copper for cutouts, overcast cutout edges of A, G and H pieces. With matching colors, overcast edges of B-D pieces.

2: For each Stand (make 3) hold four F pieces together as one and omitting attachment edge, with white, whipstitch together. Whipstitch one Stand to center of each E and I pieces as indicated on graphs.

3: With copper, holding Backs to wrong side of corresponding Fronts, whipstitch together, leaving opening at tops for photo insert. Overcast unfinished edges.

NOTE: Cut wire into one 1-yd. [0.9m] and two ½-yd. [0.5m] lengths.

4: For Hearts #1-#3, using 1-yd. length of wire for B, thread beads of choice onto wire. Wrap wire around B as desired. Repeat using remaining beads, wire pieces and C and D pieces (see photo).

5: Glue Hearts #1-#3 to Front of Wired Heart Frame as shown. Insert photos inside Frames and display as desired.

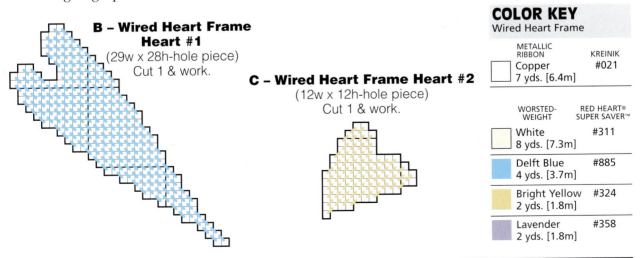

B – Wired Heart Frame Heart #1
(29w x 28h-hole piece)
Cut 1 & work.

C – Wired Heart Frame Heart #2
(12w x 12h-hole piece)
Cut 1 & work.

A – Wired Heart Frame Front
(38w x 34h-hole piece) Cut 1 & work.

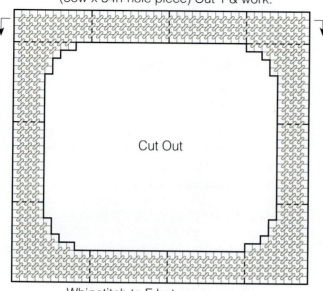

Cut Out

Whipstitch to E between arrows.

COLOR KEY
Heart Shaped Frame

	METALLIC RIBBON	KREINIK
☐	Copper 5 yds. [4.6m]	#021

	WORSTED-WEIGHT	RED HEART® SUPER SAVER™
	White 5 yds. [4.6m]	#311
	Spruce 2 yds. [1.8m]	#362
	Delft Blue 1 yd. [0.9m]	#885
	Lavender 1 yd. [0.9m]	#358
	Raspberry 1 yd. [0.9m]	#375

F – Stand Piece
(14w x 28h-hole pieces)
Cut 12 & leave unworked.

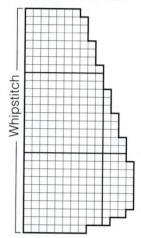

Whipstitch

E – Wired Heart Frame & Open Heart Frame Back
(38w x 33h-hole pieces) Cut 1 each & leave unworked.

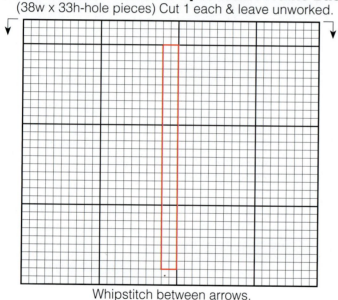

Whipstitch between arrows.

D – Wired Heart Frame Heart #3
(12w x 12h-hole piece)
Cut 1 & work.

ATTACHMENT
☐ Stand/Back

COLOR KEY
Wired Heart Frame

	METALLIC RIBBON	KREINIK
☐	Copper 7 yds. [6.4m]	#021

	WORSTED-WEIGHT	RED HEART® SUPER SAVER™
	White 8 yds. [7.3m]	#311
	Delft Blue 4 yds. [3.7m]	#885
	Bright Yellow 2 yds. [1.8m]	#324
	Lavender 2 yds. [1.8m]	#358

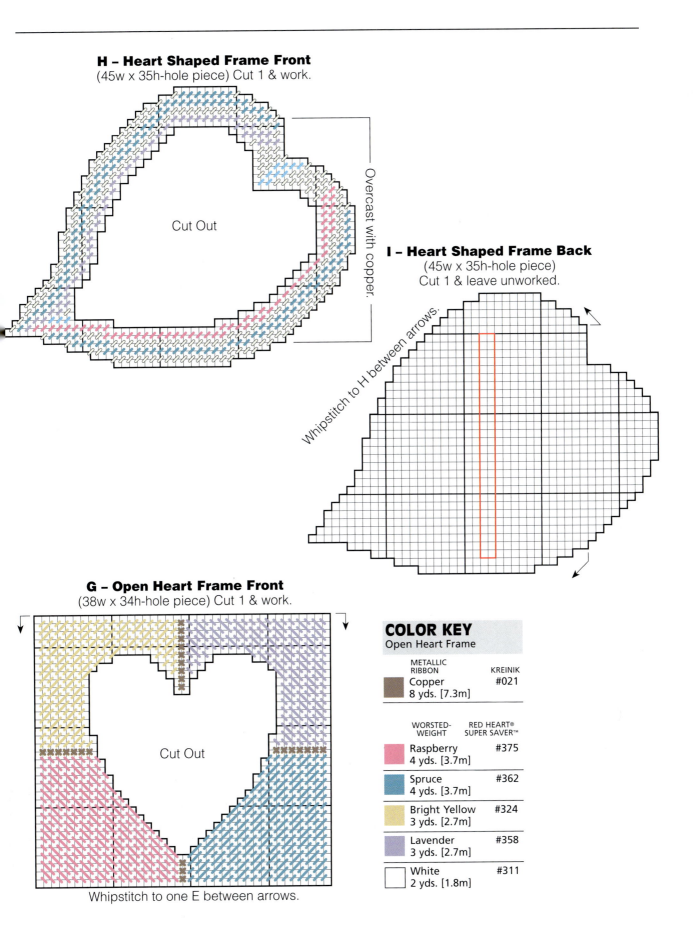

H – Heart Shaped Frame Front
(45w x 35h-hole piece) Cut 1 & work.

Cut Out

Overcast with copper.

I – Heart Shaped Frame Back
(45w x 35h-hole piece)
Cut 1 & leave unworked.

Whipstitch to H between arrows.

G – Open Heart Frame Front
(38w x 34h-hole piece) Cut 1 & work.

Cut Out

Whipstitch to one E between arrows.

COLOR KEY
Open Heart Frame

METALLIC RIBBON	KREINIK
Copper 8 yds. [7.3m]	#021

WORSTED-WEIGHT	RED HEART® SUPER SAVER™
Raspberry 4 yds. [3.7m]	#375
Spruce 4 yds. [3.7m]	#362
Bright Yellow 3 yds. [2.7m]	#324
Lavender 3 yds. [2.7m]	#358
White 2 yds. [1.8m]	#311

Holiday Candy Cups

Designed by Dorothy Tabor

*Having a party? Use these cute cups as decorations and then
give them away as favors as your guests depart.*

SIZES

Snowman Cup is 2" x 4" x 5⅛" tall [5.1cm x 10.2cm x 13cm]; Bunny Cup is 2½" x 4" x 6" tall [6.4cm x 10.2cm x 15.2cm]; Halloween Cup is 2" x 4¼" x 6¼" tall [5.1cm x 10.8cm x 15.9cm]; Pumpkin Patch Cup is 1½" x 4⅜" x 4⅝" tall [3.8cm x 11.1cm x 11.7cm]; Goose Cup is 1¾" x 4¼" x 5¾" tall [4.4cm x 10.8cm x 14.6cm]; July 4th Cup is 1⅞" x 5" x 3⅞" tall [4.8cm x 12.7cm x 9.8cm].

MATERIALS FOR ONE

- One sheet of 7-mesh plastic canvas
- One 5mm gold sequin (for Snowman Cup)
- Six-strand embroidery floss (for amounts see individual Color Keys)
- Worsted-weight or plastic canvas yarn (for amounts see individual Color Keys).

SNOWMAN CUP

CUTTING INSTRUCTIONS

A: For Snowman Back, cut one according to graph.

B: For Snowman Front, cut one according to graph.

C: For Snowman Sides, cut two 8w x 14h-holes (no graph).

D: For Snowman Bottom, cut one 12w x 8h-holes (no graph).

E: For Snowman Arms, cut one according to graph.

F: For Snowman Feet, cut one according to graph.

STITCHING INSTRUCTIONS

NOTE: D is not worked.

1: Using colors and stitches indicated, work A, B, E and F pieces according to graphs; with white and continental stitch, work C pieces. Omitting attachment area, with matching colors, overcast edges of E and F pieces.

2: Using 6 strands floss and yarn in colors and embroi-dery stitches indicated, embroider detail on A as indicated on graph.

3: With white, whipstitch A-D pieces together as indicated on graph, forming Snowman Cup; with black whipstitch F to bottom Front of Cup (see photo). With matching colors, overcast unfinished edges.

4: Glue wrong side of Arms to wrong side of Snowman Back, wrap Arms around Snowman Front and glue to secure (see photo). Glue gold sequin to hat as shown.

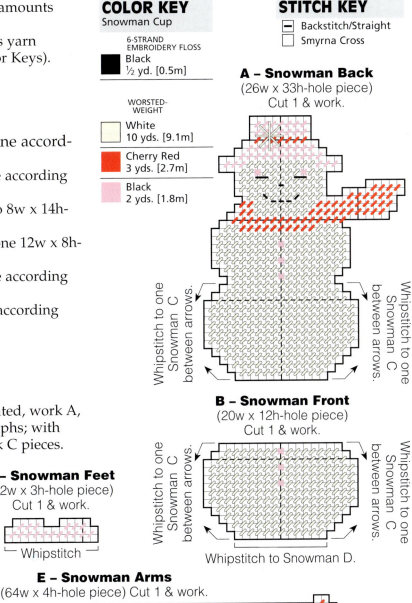

COLOR KEY
Snowman Cup

	6-STRAND EMBROIDERY FLOSS	
■	Black	½ yd. [0.5m]

	WORSTED-WEIGHT	
□	White	10 yds. [9.1m]
■	Cherry Red	3 yds. [2.7m]
■	Black	2 yds. [1.8m]

STITCH KEY
- ⊟ Backstitch/Straight
- ☐ Smyrna Cross

A – Snowman Back
(26w x 33h-hole piece)
Cut 1 & work.

Whipstitch to one Snowman C between arrows.

Whipstitch to one Snowman C between arrows.

B – Snowman Front
(20w x 12h-hole piece)
Cut 1 & work.

Whipstitch to one Snowman C between arrows.

Whipstitch to one Snowman C between arrows.

Whipstitch to Snowman D.

F – Snowman Feet
(12w x 3h-hole piece)
Cut 1 & work.

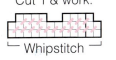

Whipstitch

E – Snowman Arms
(64w x 4h-hole piece) Cut 1 & work.

BUNNY CUP

CUTTING INSTRUCTIONS

A: For Bunny Back, cut one according to graph.

B: For Bunny Front, cut one according to graph.

C: For Bunny Side #1, cut one 8w x 17h-holes; for Bunny Side #2, cut one 8w x 13h-holes.

D: For Bunny Bottom, cut one 13w x 8h-holes (no graph).

E: For Bunny Arms, cut one according to graph.

F: For Bunny Feet, cut two according to graphs.

STITCHING INSTRUCTIONS
NOTE: D is not worked.

1: Using colors and stitches indicated, work A-C, E and F pieces according to graphs; Omitting attachment area, with white, overcast edges of E and F pieces.

2: Using 6 strands floss and yarn (Separate into individual plies, if desired.) in colors and embroidery stitches indicated, embroider detail on A as indicated on graph.

3: With purple, whipstitch A-D pieces together as indicated, forming Bunny Cup; with white whipstitch F pieces to bottom Front of Cup (see photo). With matching colors, overcast unfinished edges.

4: Glue wrong side of Arms to wrong side of Bunny Back; wrap Arms around Bunny Front and glue to secure (see photo).

A – Bunny Back
(21w x 38h-hole piece)
Cut 1 & work.

Whipstitch to one Bunny C#1.

Whipstitch to one Bunny C#2.

B – Bunny Front
(21w x 18h-hole piece) Cut 1 & work.

Whipstitch to Bunny C#1.

Whipstitch to Bunny C#2.

Whipstitch to Bunny D.

C – Bunny Side #1
(8w x 17h-hole piece)
Cut 1 & work.

Whipstitch to Bunny A.

Whipstitch to Bunny B.

Whipstitch to Bunny D.

F – Bunny Feet
(10w x 5h-hole pieces)
Cut 2. Work 1 & 1 reversed.

Whipstitch

C – Bunny Side #2
(8w x 13h-hole piece)
Cut 1 & work.

Whipstitch to Bunny B.

Whipstitch to Bunny A.

Whipstitch to Bunny D.

E – Bunny Arms
(61w x 5h-hole piece) Cut 1 & work.

COLOR KEY
Bunny Cup

6-STRAND EMBROIDERY FLOSS	
Black	1 yd. [0.9m]
WORSTED-WEIGHT	
White	10 yds. [9.1m]
Purple	8 yds. [7.3m]
Yellow	2 yds. [1.8m]
Lilac	1 yd. [0.9m]
Black	¼ yd. [0.2m]
Pink	¼ yd. [0.2m]

STITCH KEY

⊟ Backstitch/Straight

HALLOWEEN CUP

CUTTING INSTRUCTIONS

A: For Halloween Back, cut one according to graph.

B: For Halloween Front, cut one according to graph.

C: For Halloween Sides, cut two 10w x 16h-holes (no graphs).

D: For Halloween Bottom, cut one 20w x 10h-holes (no graph).

E: For Halloween Pumpkin, cut one according to graph.

STITCHING INSTRUCTIONS
NOTE: D is not worked.

1: Using colors and stitches indicated, work A, B and E pieces according to graphs; work C pieces using black yarn and continental stitch. Omitting attachment area, with matching colors, overcast edges of E.

2: Using 6 strands floss in colors and embroidery stitches indicated, embroider detail on A, B and E pieces as indicated on graphs.

3: With black, whipstitch A-D pieces together as indicated, forming Halloween Cup; with orange whipstitch E to bottom Front of Cup (see photo). With matching colors, overcast unfinished edges.

COLOR KEY
Halloween Cup

6-STRAND EMBROIDERY FLOSS

	Black 2 yds. [1.8m]
	Gold 2 yds. [1.8m]
	Red ¼ yd. [0.2m]

WORSTED-WEIGHT

	Black 12 yds. [11m]
	White 5 yds. [4.6m]
	Orange 2 yds. [1.8m]
	Green ¼ yd. [0.2m]

STITCH KEY

− Backstitch/Straight

E – Halloween Pumpkin
(14w x 12h-hole piece)
Cut 1 & work.

Whipstitch

A – Halloween Back
(30w x 41h-hole piece) Cut 1 & work.

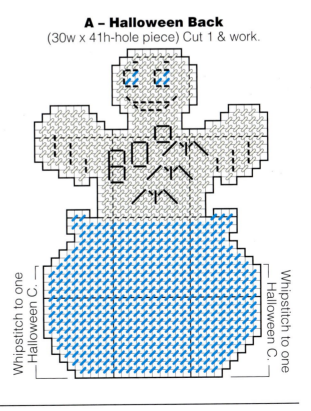

B – Halloween Front
(28w x 21h-hole piece)
Cut 1 & work.

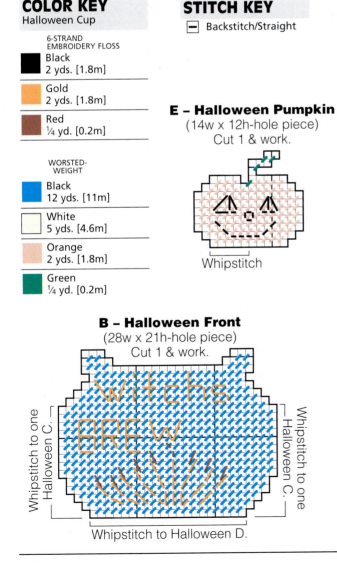

Whipstitch to one Halloween C.

Whipstitch to one Halloween C.

Whipstitch to Halloween D.

Whipstitch to one Halloween C.

Whipstitch to one Halloween C.

PUMPKIN PATCH CUP

CUTTING INSTRUCTIONS

A: For Pumpkin Patch Back, cut one according to graph.

B: For Pumpkin Patch Front, cut one according to graph.

C: For Pumpkin Patch Sides, cut two 8w x 14h-holes (no graphs).

D: For Pumpkin Patch Bottom, cut one 18w x 8h-holes (no graph).

E: For Pumpkin Patch Pumpkin, cut one according to graph.

STITCHING INSTRUCTIONS

NOTE: D is not worked.

1: Using colors and stitches indicated, work A, B and E pieces according to graphs; work C pieces using orange and continental stitch. Omitting attachment area, with matching colors, overcast cutout edges of A and outer edges of E.

2: Using 3 strands black floss and embroidery stitches indicated, embroider detail on A, B and E pieces as indicated on graphs.

3: With orange, whipstitch A-D pieces together as indicated, forming Pumpkin Patch Cup; whipstitch E to bottom Front of Cup (see photo). With matching colors, overcast unfinished edges.

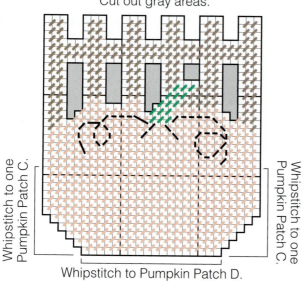

A – Pumpkin Patch Back
(28w x 30h-hole piece) Cut 1 & work.
Cut out gray areas.

Whipstitch to one Pumpkin Patch C.

Whipstitch to one Pumpkin Patch C.

Whipstitch to Pumpkin Patch D.

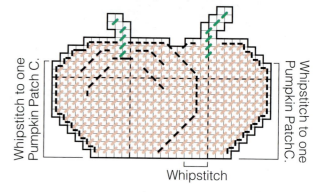

B – Pumpkin Patch Front
(28w x 19h-hole piece) Cut 1 & work.

Whipstitch to one Pumpkin Patch C.

Whipstitch to one Pumpkin Patch C.

Whipstitch

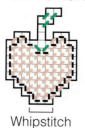

E – Pumpkin Patch Pumpkin
(9w x 12h-hole piece)
Cut 1 & work.

Whipstitch

STITCH KEY
— Backstitch/Straight

COLOR KEY
Pumpkin Patch Cup

3-STRAND EMBROIDERY FLOSS
■ Black 2 yds. [1.8m]

WORSTED-WEIGHT
Orange 12 yds. [11m]
Green 5 yds. [4.6m]
Tan 5 yds. [4.6m]

GOOSE CUP

CUTTING INSTRUCTIONS

A: For Goose Sides, cut two according to graph.

B: For Goose End #1 and #2, cut one 10w x 20h-holes for End #1 and one 10w x 12h-holes for End #2.

C: For Goose Wings, cut two according to graph.

D: For Goose Bottom, cut one 10w x 15h-holes (no graph).

STITCHING INSTRUCTIONS

NOTE: D is not worked.

1: Using colors and stitches indicated, work A and C pieces according to graphs; work B pieces using white and continental stitch. With matching colors, overcast edges of C pieces.

2: Using 6-strand black floss and embroidery stitches indicated, embroider detail on A and C pieces as indicated on graphs.

3: With eggshell, whipstitch A, B and D pieces together as indicated, forming Goose Cup; with matching colors, overcast unfinished edges.

NOTE: Cut a 9" [22.9cm] length of red yarn.

4: Glue one Wing to each Side (see photo). Insert yarn through each u hole on Sides; tie into a knot and fray ends as desired.

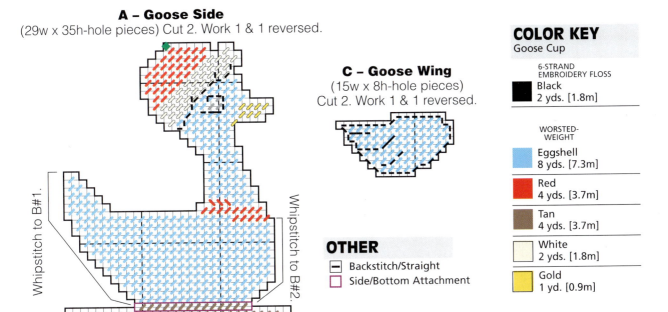

A – Goose Side
(29w x 35h-hole pieces) Cut 2. Work 1 & 1 reversed.

Whipstitch to B#1.

Whipstitch to B#2.

C – Goose Wing
(15w x 8h-hole pieces)
Cut 2. Work 1 & 1 reversed.

OTHER
- ▬ Backstitch/Straight
- ☐ Side/Bottom Attachment

COLOR KEY
Goose Cup

6-STRAND EMBROIDERY FLOSS
- ■ Black 2 yds. [1.8m]

WORSTED-WEIGHT
- ■ Eggshell 8 yds. [7.3m]
- ■ Red 4 yds. [3.7m]
- ■ Tan 4 yds. [3.7m]
- ☐ White 2 yds. [1.8m]
- ■ Gold 1 yd. [0.9m]

JULY 4TH CUP

CUTTING INSTRUCTIONS

A: For July 4th Back, cut one according to graph.

B: For July 4th Front, cut one according to graph.

C: For July 4th Sides, cut two 10w x 12h-holes.

D: For July 4th Bottom, cut one 32w x 10h-holes (no graph).

E: For July 4th Base Ends, cut two 10w x 4h-holes (no graphs).

F: For July 4th Base Tops, cut two 6w x 10h-holes (no graphs).

G: For July 4th Band, cut one 18w x 4h-holes.

H: For July 4th Top, cut one 18w x 10h-holes.

I: For July 4th Top Ends, cut two 10w x 8h-holes (no graphs).

J: For July 4th Top Front, cut one 18w x 8h-holes (no graph).

STITCHING INSTRUCTIONS
NOTE: D is not worked.

1: Using colors and stitches indicated, work A-C, G, and H pieces according to graphs; work E and F pieces using red and diagonal stitch. Work I and J pieces using pattern established on H piece. Omitting attachment edges, with matching colors, overcast edges of G.

2: Using white and smyrna cross, embroider detail on G as indicated on graph.

3: Whipstitch A-I together according to July 4th Assembly Diagram.

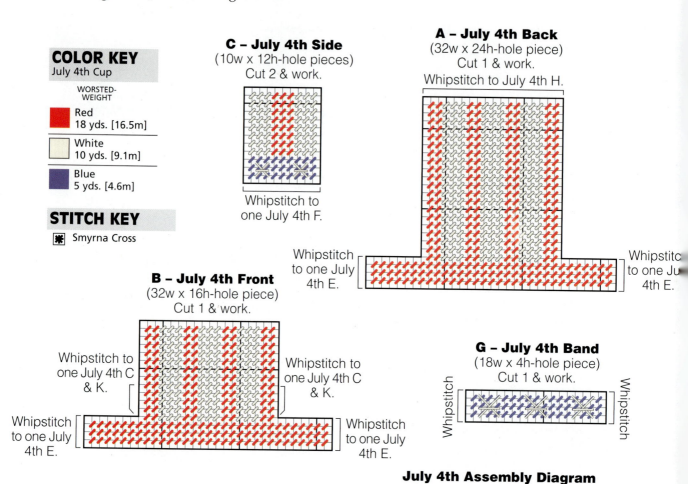

COLOR KEY
July 4th Cup

WORSTED-WEIGHT

Red
18 yds. [16.5m]

White
10 yds. [9.1m]

Blue
5 yds. [4.6m]

STITCH KEY

Smyrna Cross

C – July 4th Side
(10w x 12h-hole pieces)
Cut 2 & work.

Whipstitch to one July 4th F.

A – July 4th Back
(32w x 24h-hole piece)
Cut 1 & work.
Whipstitch to July 4th H.

Whipstitch to one July 4th E.

Whipstitch to one July 4th E.

B – July 4th Front
(32w x 16h-hole piece)
Cut 1 & work.

Whipstitch to one July 4th C & K.

Whipstitch to one July 4th C & K.

Whipstitch to one July 4th E.

Whipstitch to one July 4th E.

G – July 4th Band
(18w x 4h-hole piece)
Cut 1 & work.

Whipstitch

Whipstitch

H – July 4th Top
(18w x 10h-hole piece)
Cut 1 & work.
Whipstitch to July 4th A.

Whipstitch to one July 4th I.

Whipstitch to one July 4th I.

July 4th Assembly Diagram
(Pieces are shown in different colors for contrast; gray denotes wrong side.)

Step 1:
With red, whipstitch A-F pieces together; with blue, whipstitch G to B.

Step 2:
With red, whipstitch H-J pieces together & to A.

Step 3:
With red, overcast unfinished edges.

Kitchen Quilts

Designed by Pam Bull

Bring the hominess of old-fashioned quilts to your kitchen.

SIZES

Napkin Holder is 3" x 7½" x 3½" tall [7.6cm x 19cm x 8.9cm]; Napkin Ring is 1¼" across x 2¼" tall [3.2cm x 5.7cm]; Switchplate Cover is 3" x 5¼" [7.6cm x 13.3cm]; Teabag Holder is 2½" x 4¼" x 2½" tall [6.4cm x 10.8cm x 6.4cm].

MATERIALS

- Two sheets of 7-mesh plastic canvas
- Two 12" x 12" [30.5cm x 30.5cm] sheets of tan felt
- 2 yds. of ¼" [6mm] ecru lace
- Two 2" [5.1cm] Velcro® strips
- Craft glue or glue gun
- Chenille yarn (for amount see Color Key)
- Worsted-weight or plastic canvas yarn (for amounts see Color Key).

CUTTING INSTRUCTIONS

A: For Napkin Holder Sides, cut two 49w x 21h-holes.

B: For Napkin Holder Ends, cut two 19w x 15h-holes.

C: For Napkin Holder Bottom, cut one 49w x 19h-holes (no graph).

D: For Napkin Ring, cut one 29w x 13h-holes.

E: For Switchplate Cover, cut one according to graph.

F: For Teabag Holder Sides, cut two 27w x 15h-holes.

G: For Teabag Holder Ends, cut two 15w x 15h-holes.

H: For Teabag Holder Bottom, cut one 27w x 15h-holes (no graph).

I: For Linings, using A-C and F-H pieces as patterns, cut one each from felt ⅛" [3mm] smaller at all edges.

STITCHING INSTRUCTIONS

NOTE: C, H and I pieces are not worked.

1: Using colors and stitches indicated, work A, B and D-G pieces according to graphs; omitting attachment edges, with aran, overcast cutout on E and edges of A, B, D and E pieces.

2: With aran, whipstitch A-C pieces together as indicated on graph, forming Napkin Holder; whipstitch ends of D together as indicated, forming Napkin Ring. Whipstitch F-H pieces together, forming Teabag Holder. Overcast all unfinished edges of each assembly.

3: Glue Linings to wrong side of corresponding pieces. Glue lace around bottom of Napkin Holder and Teabag Holder and to Switchplate Cover and Napkin Ring, trimming ends to fit (see photo). Adhere Velcro® strips to wrong side of Switchplate Cover.

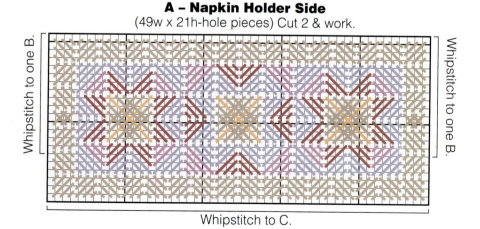

A – Napkin Holder Side
(49w x 21h-hole pieces) Cut 2 & work.

Whipstitch to one B.

Whipstitch to one B.

Whipstitch to C.

F – Teabag Holder Side
(27w x 15h-hole pieces) Cut 2 & work.

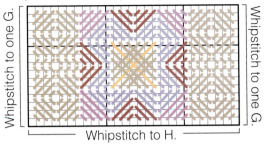

Whipstitch to one G.

Whipstitch to one G.

Whipstitch to H.

B – Napkin Holder End
(19w x 15h-hole pieces)
Cut 2 & work.

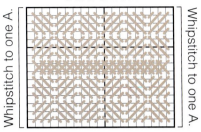

Whipstitch to one A.

Whipstitch to one A.

G – Teabag Holder End
(15w x 15h-hole pieces)
Cut 2 & work.

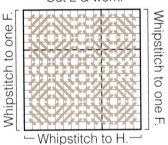

Whipstitch to one F.

Whipstitch to one F.

Whipstitch to H.

E – Switchplate Cover
(19w x 33h-hole piece) Cut 1 & work.
Cut out gray area.

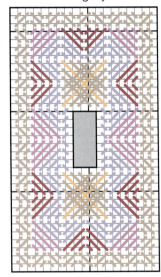

COLOR KEY
Kitchen Quilts

	CHENILLE YARN	LION BRAND®
Brick	3 yds. [2.7m]	#134

	WORSTED-WEIGHT	
Aran	47 yds. [43m]	
Venice	16 yds. [14.6m]	
Camel	8 yds. [7.3m]	
Lilac	8 yds. [7.3m]	

D – Napkin Ring
(29w x 13h-hole piece) Cut 1 & work.

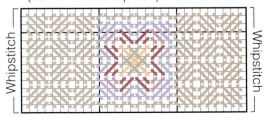

Whipstitch

Whipstitch

Starry Night

Designed by Joan Green

This Starry Night can be used year-round to remind us of our blessed Saviour's birth.

SIZE

7½" x 11¼" [19.1cm x 28.6cm], not including hanger.

MATERIALS

- One sheet of 7-mesh plastic canvas
- Twelve yellow 15mm star-shaped faceted gemstones
- Twelve topaz 15mm star-shaped faceted gemstones
- One 12" [30.5cm] gold glitter stem
- Craft glue or glue gun
- Metallic plastic canvas yarn (for amounts see Color Key)
- Worsted-weight or plastic canvas yarn (for amounts see Color Key).

CUTTING INSTRUCTIONS

For Starry Night, cut one according to graph.

STITCHING INSTRUCTIONS

1: Using colors and stitches indicated, work piece according to graph; with dk. gold, overcast edges.

2: Using metallic and worsted yarn in colors and embroidery stitches indicated, embroider detail on piece as indicated on graph.

3: Glue gemstones to front as desired or as shown in photo.

4: For hanger, glue ends of glitter stem to wrong side of piece as shown.

Starry Night
(50w x 75h-hole piece) Cut 1 & work.

COLOR KEY
Starry Night

	METALLIC YARN	RAINBOW GALLERY
	Midnight Blue 17 yds. [15.5m]	#PC26
	Black 8 yds. [7.3m]	#PM61
	Dk. Gold 7 yds. [6.4m]	#PC18
	Yellow Gold 7 yds. [6.4m]	#PC7

	WORSTED-WEIGHT	RED HEART-CLASSIC®
	Olympic Blue 18 yds. [16.5m]	#849
	Lt. Sage 5 yds. [4.6m]	#631
	Blue Jewel 4 yds. [3.7m]	#818
	True Blue 3 yds. [2.7m]	#822
	Med. Clay 2 yds. [1.8m]	#280
	Warm Brown 2 yds. [1.8m]	#336
	Coffee 1 yd. [0.9m]	#365
	Off White 1 yd. [0.9m]	#3
	Sea Coral 1 yd. [0.9m]	#246

STITCH KEY
- Backstitch/Straight
- French Knot

Holly Holiday Frame

Designed by Kristine Loffredo

Personalize your wreath this year with this holly-day frame!

SIZE
12" x 16" [30.5cm x 40.6cm].

MATERIALS
- Two 13½" x 22½" [34.3cm x 57.2cm] sheets of 7-mesh plastic canvas
- Seven red 8mm facet beads
- Five photos of choice
- Craft glue or glue gun
- Craft cord (for amount see Color Key)
- Worsted-weight or plastic canvas yarn (for amounts see Color Key).

CUTTING INSTRUCTIONS
A: For Bow, cut one according to graph.

B: For Bow Center, cut one according to graph.

C: For Frame Front, cut one according to graph.

D: For Frame Backing, cut one according to graph.

E: For Holly Leaves, cut seven according to graph.

STITCHING INSTRUCTIONS
NOTE: D is not worked.

1: Using colors and stitches indicated, work A-C and E pieces according to graphs; with cord for cutouts and with matching colors, overcast indicated edges of A and edges of B and E pieces.

2: With matching colors, whipstitch Backing to wrong side of Front as indicated, leaving openings for photo inserts.

3: Fold ends of Bow wrong sides together and tack to center of Bow working through all thicknesses.

4: Glue Bow Center to center of Bow and Holly leaves to Frame Front as shown in photo. Glue one bead to center of each Holly Leaf.

5: Display or hang as desired.

B – Bow Center
(5w x 5h-hole piece)
Cut 1 & work.

E – Holly Leaves
(19w x 9h-hole pieces)
Cut 7 & work.

COLOR KEY
Holly Holiday Frame

	CRAFT CORD	NEED-LOFT®
☐	Gold 5 yds. [4.6m]	#01

	WORSTED-WEIGHT	NEED-LOFT®
🟥	Red 22 yds. [20.1m]	#01
🟩	Holly 11 yds. [10.1m]	#27
🟧	Br. Orange 5 yds. [4.6m]	#58
🟪	Br. Pink 5 yds. [4.6m]	#62
🟦	Br. Purple 5 yds. [4.6m]	#64
🟦	Royal 5 yds. [4.6m]	#32
🟨	Yellow 5 yds. [4.6m]	#57

A – Bow
(88w x 12h-hole piece) Cut 1 & work; leaving uncoded area unworked.

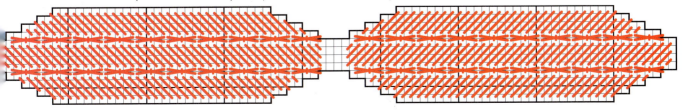

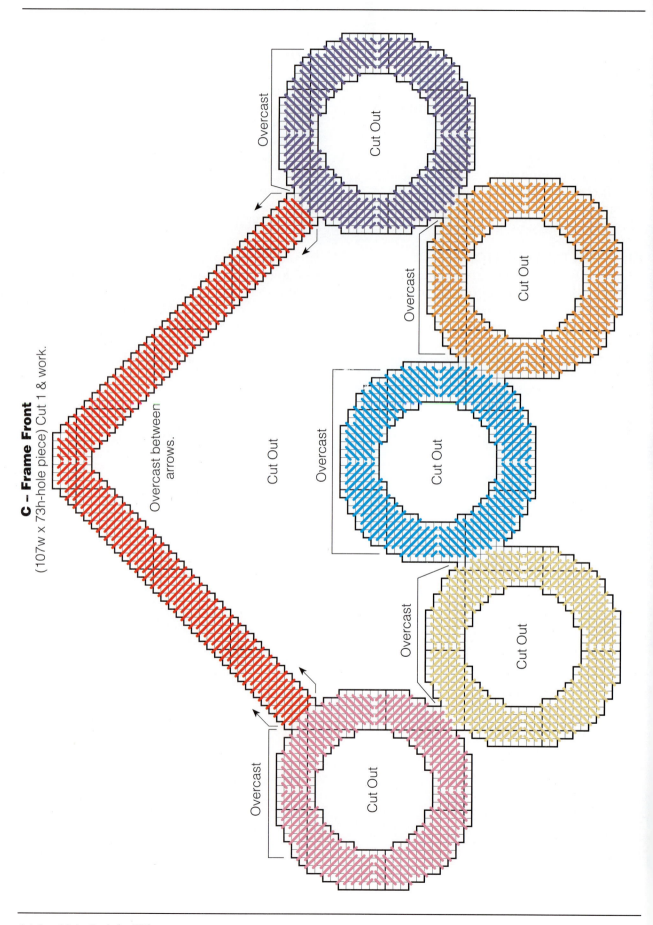

C – Frame Front

(107w x 73h-hole piece) Cut 1 & work.

Overcast between arrows.

Overcast

Cut Out

Overcast

Cut Out

Cut Out

Overcast

Cut Out

Overcast

Cut Out

Overcast

Cut Out

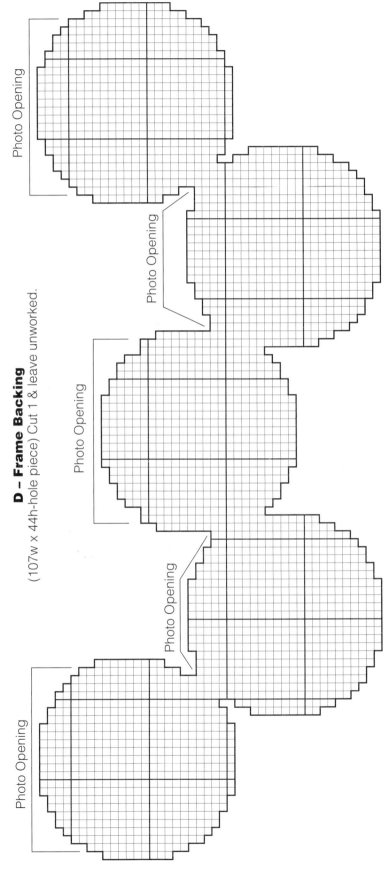

COLOR KEY
Holly Holiday Frame

CRAFT CORD	NEED-LOFT®	
Gold 5 yds. [4.6m]	#01	

WORSTED-WEIGHT	NEED-LOFT®	
Red 22 yds. [20.1m]	#01	
Holly 11 yds. [10.1m]	#27	
Br. Orange 5 yds. [4.6m]	#58	
Br. Pink 5 yds. [4.6m]	#62	
Br. Purple 5 yds. [4.6m]	#64	
Royal 5 yds. [4.6m]	#32	
Yellow 5 yds. [4.6m]	#57	

D – Frame Backing
(107w x 44h-hole piece) Cut 1 & leave unworked.

Photo Opening

Photo Opening

Photo Opening

Photo Opening

Memo Cube Holders

Designed by Judy Collishaw

Always have a note handy with these clever note pad holders.

SIZES

Pastry Pup is 3½" x 3½" x 7½" tall [8.9cm x 8.9cm x 19.1cm] and holds a 3¼" square [8.3cm] memo cube;
Harried Housewife is 3½" x 3½" x 5¾" tall [8.9cm x 8.9m x 14.6cm] and holds a 3¼" [8.3cm] square memo cube.

PASTRY PUP

MATERIALS
• One sheet of 7-mesh plastic canvas
• Two black 5mm round beads
• Beading needle and monofilament thread
• Craft glue or glue gun
• No. 5 pearl cotton or six-strand embroidery floss (for amounts see Color Key)
• Worsted-weight or plastic canvas yarn (for amounts see Color Key).

CUTTING INSTRUCTIONS
   A: For Body Front, cut one according to graph.
   B: For Body Back, cut one according to graph.
   C: For Sides, cut two 23w x 19h-holes.
   D: For Front Pieces, cut two 6w x 19h-holes.
   E: For Bottom, cut one 23w x 23h-holes (no graph).
   F: For Muzzle, cut one according to graph.
   G: For Front Paws, cut two according to graph.
   H: For Back Paws, cut two according to graph.
   I: For Measuring Cup, cut one according to graph.
   J: For Rolling Pin, cut one according to graph.
   K: For Hat, cut two according to graph.

STITCHING INSTRUCTIONS
NOTE: E is not worked.

1: Using colors and stitches indicated, work A-D and F-K pieces according to graphs. With matching colors, overcast indicated edge of A and edges of F, G, I and J pieces; with brown, overcast edges of H pieces.

2: Using pearl cotton or six strands floss and yarn (Separate yarn into individual plies, if desired.) in colors and embroidery stitches indicated, embroider detail on G-I and K pieces as indicated on graphs.

3: Using beading needle and monofilament thread, sew beads to A as indicated.

4: With matching colors, whipstitch A-E pieces together according to Memo Cube Assembly Illustration; overcast unfinished edges.

5: With white, whipstitch K pieces wrong sides together as indicated, forming Hat; overcast unfinished edges. Slip Hat over head as shown in photo; glue to secure.

6: Glue Muzzle to Body Front as shown; glue Measuring Cup, Rolling Pin, Front Paws and Back Paws to Front Pieces as shown.

HARRIED HOUSEWIFE

MATERIALS
• One sheet of 7-mesh plastic canvas
• Two black 4mm round beads
• Beading needle and monofilament thread
• 6" [15.2cm] miniature mop
• 2" [5.1cm] miniature wire clothes hanger
• Craft glue or glue gun
• No. 5 pearl cotton or six-strand embroidery floss (for amount see Color Key)
• Worsted-weight or plastic canvas yarn (for amounts see Color Key).

CUTTING INSTRUCTIONS
   A: For Body Front, cut one according to graph.
   B: For Body Back, cut one according to graph.
   C: For Sides, cut two 23w x 19h-holes.
   D: For Front Pieces, cut two 6w x 19h-holes.
   E: For Bottom, cut one 23w x 23h-holes (no graph).
   F: For Hands, cut two according to graph.

STITCHING INSTRUCTIONS
NOTE: E is not worked.

1: Using colors and stitches indicated, work A (See modified turkey work stitch illustration; leave ¼" [6mm] loops.), B-D and F pieces according to graphs. With matching colors, overcast indicated edge of A and edges of F pieces.

2: Using pearl cotton or six strands floss and backstitch, embroider detail on A as indicated on graph.

3: Using beading needle and monofilament thread, sew beads to A as indicated.

4: With matching colors, whipstitch A-E pieces together according to Memo Cube Assembly Illustration; overcast unfinished edges.

5: Glue clothes hanger, mop and Hands to Front Pieces as shown in photo.

NOTE: Cut one 9" [22.9cm] length each of red and white yarn; tie each length into a bow.

6: Glue red bow to top of head as shown; glue white bow to Body Back as indicated.

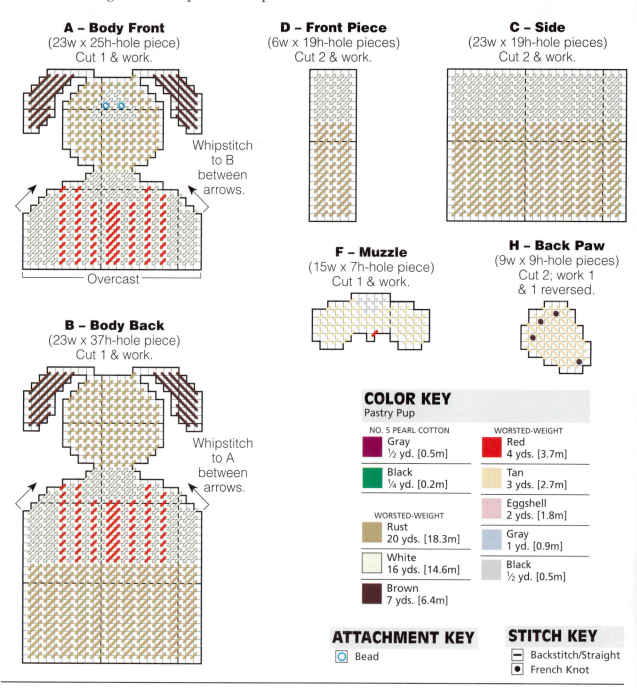

A – Body Front
(23w x 25h-hole piece)
Cut 1 & work.

Whipstitch to B between arrows.

Overcast

B – Body Back
(23w x 37h-hole piece)
Cut 1 & work.

Whipstitch to A between arrows.

D – Front Piece
(6w x 19h-hole pieces)
Cut 2 & work.

C – Side
(23w x 19h-hole pieces)
Cut 2 & work.

F – Muzzle
(15w x 7h-hole piece)
Cut 1 & work.

H – Back Paw
(9w x 9h-hole pieces)
Cut 2; work 1 & 1 reversed.

COLOR KEY
Pastry Pup

NO. 5 PEARL COTTON
- Gray ½ yd. [0.5m]
- Black ¼ yd. [0.2m]

WORSTED-WEIGHT
- Rust 20 yds. [18.3m]
- White 16 yds. [14.6m]
- Brown 7 yds. [6.4m]

WORSTED-WEIGHT
- Red 4 yds. [3.7m]
- Tan 3 yds. [2.7m]
- Eggshell 2 yds. [1.8m]
- Gray 1 yd. [0.9m]
- Black ½ yd. [0.5m]

ATTACHMENT KEY
- O Bead

STITCH KEY
- ─ Backstitch/Straight
- • French Knot

G – Front Paw
(8w x 8h-hole pieces)
Cut 2; work 1
& 1 reversed.

I – Measuring Cup
(10w x 6h-hole piece)
Cut 1 & work.

J – Rolling Pin
(22w x 4h-hole piece)
Cut 1 & work.

K – Hat
(13w x 14h-hole pieces)
Cut 2; work 1 & 1 reversed.

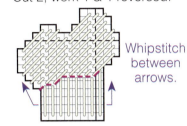

Whipstitch between arrows.

Memo Cube Assembly Illustration
(Pieces are shown in different colors for contrast; gray denotes wrong side.)

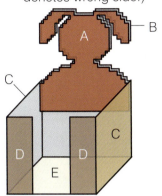

A – Body Front
(23w x 26h-hole piece)
Cut 1 & work.

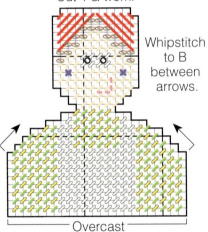

Whipstitch to B between arrows.

Overcast

F – Hand
(7w x 6h-hole pieces)
Cut 2; work 1 & 1 reversed.

STITCH KEY
− Backstitch/Straight
⊘ Modified Turkey Work

ATTACHMENT KEY
◻ Bead

PLACEMENT KEY
◇ White Bow/Body Back

B – Body Back
(23w x 37h-hole piece)
Cut 1 & work.

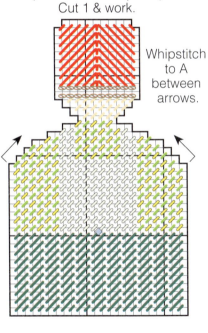

Whipstitch to A between arrows.

C – Side
(23w x 19h-hole pieces)
Cut 2 & work.

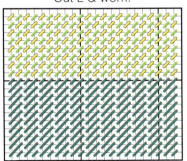

D – Front Piece
(6w x 19h-hole pieces)
Cut 2 & work.

COLOR KEY
Harried Housewife

NO. 5 PEARL COTTON	WORSTED-WEIGHT
▦ Red ½ yd. [0.5m]	▢ White 4 yds. [3.7m]
WORSTED-WEIGHT	▦ Peach 3½ yds. [3.2m]
▦ Dark Forest 14 yds. [12.8m]	▦ Medium Brown 3 yds. [2.7m]
▦ Yellow 10 yds. [9.1m]	▦ Red 3 yds. [2.7m]
▦ Lime 8 yds. 7.3m]	▦ Rose ½ yd. [0.5m]

Happy Gardener

Designed by Janelle Giese

Stitch this Happy Gardener for the horticulturist in your family.

SIZE
3" x 7" x 6½" tall [7.6cm x 17.8cm x 16.5cm].

MATERIALS
- One sheet of 7-mesh plastic canvas
- No. 5 pearl cotton (coton perlé) (for amount see Color Key)
- Six-strand embroidery floss (for amount see Color Key)
- Worsted-weight or plastic canvas yarn (for amounts see Color Key).

CUTTING INSTRUCTIONS
  A: For Front, cut one according to graph.
  B: For Back, cut one according to graph.
  C: For Sides, cut two according to graph.
  D: For Bottom, cut one 33w x 19h-holes (no graph).

STITCHING INSTRUCTIONS

1: Using colors and stitches indicated, omitting attachment areas, work A-C according to graphs; work D using forest and continental stitch. With baby blue, overcast cutouts on A-C pieces.

2: Using pearl cotton, 3 strands floss and yarn (Separate into individual plies, if desired.) in colors and embroidery stitches indicated, embroider detail on Front as indicated on graph.

3: Using baby blue for fence posts, forest for Bottom and with indicated and matching colors, whipstitch A-D pieces together.

With baby blue for fence posts and with matching colors as shown in photo, overcast unfinished edges.

A – Front
(45w x 43h-hole piece)
Cut 1 & work.

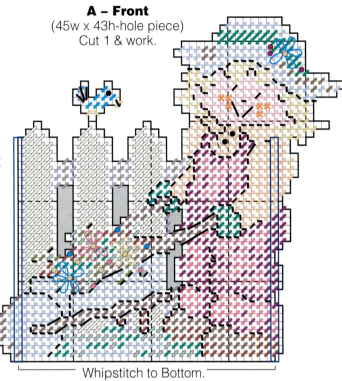

Whipstitch to Bottom.

OTHER

- ▬ Backstitch/Straight
- ● French Knot
- ◖ Lazy Daisy
- ▫ Front/Side

B – Back
(33w x 30h-hole piece)
Cut 1 & work.

C – Side
(19w x 30h-hole pieces)
Cut 2 & work.

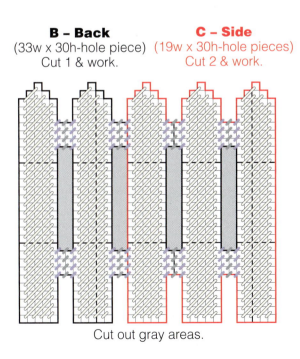

Cut out gray areas.

COLOR KEY
Happy Gardener

NO. 5 PEARL COTTON		DMC®
■ Black 7 yds. [6.4m]		#310

3-STRAND EMBROIDERY FLOSS		DMC®
■ Lt. Salmon 1 yd. [0.9m]		#761

WORSTED-WEIGHT		NEED-LOFT®
□ White 20 yds. [18.3m]		#41
■ Forest 13 yds. [11.9m]		#29
■ Baby Blue 12 yds. [11m]		#36
■ Camel 4 yds. [3.7m]		#43
■ Lavender 4 yds. [3.7m]		#05
■ Cinnamon 3 yds. [2.7m]		#14

WORSTED-WEIGHT		NEED-LOFT®
■ Eggshell 3 yds. [2.7m]		#39
■ Gray 3 yds. [2.7m]		#38
■ Beige 2 yds. [1.8m]		#40
■ Dk. Brown 2 yds. [1.8m]		#15
■ Pink 2 yds. [1.8m]		#07
■ Bt. Blue 1 yd. [0.9m]		#60
■ Christmas Green 1 yd. [0.9m]		#28
■ Fleshtone 1 yd. [0.9m]		#56
■ Moss 1 yd. [0.9m]		#25

Sunshine Mobile

Designed by Lee Lindeman

This little bebop car will give hours of pleasure to any little tyke.

SIZE
3¼ x 5½ x 2½ " [8.3cm x 14cm x 6.4cm].

MATERIALS
- One sheet of 7-mesh plastic canvas
- Four 1" [2.5cm] wooden wheels with axles
- Two red ½" [13mm] flat backed beads
- Two silver 1½" [13mm] flat backed rhinestones
- Red and black acrylic paint
- Small paint brush
- 2" [5.1cm] length of stiff wire
- One 3mm black bead
- One smilie face button
- Small amount of fiberfill
- Craft glue or glue gun
- Metallic yarn (for amount see Color Key)
- Six-strand embroidery floss (for amount see Color Key)
- Worsted-weight or plastic canvas yarn (for amounts see Color Key).

CUTTING INSTRUCTIONS
A: For Sides, cut two according to graph.
B: For Top, cut one 12w x 46h-holes.
C: For Bottom, cut one 12w x 30h-holes.
D: For Grills, cut two 19w x 2h-holes (no graphs).

STITCHING INSTRUCTIONS

1: Using colors indicated and continental stitch, work A-C pieces according to graphs. Using metallic yarn and continental stitch, work D pieces; overcast edges of D pieces.

2: Using black and embroidery stitches indicated, embroider detail on A and B pieces as indicated on graphs.

3: With gold, whipstitch A-C pieces together, stuffing with fiberfill before closing.

NOTE: Paint wheels red and axle ends black; let dry.

4: Insert axles through cutouts on Car; place one wheel on each end of each axle. Glue axle ends to axles.

5: Glue Grills, rhinestones, beads and smilie button to Car as shown in photo. For antennae, insert 3mm bead on one end of wire and opposite end of wire in back of Car (see photo), glue to secure.

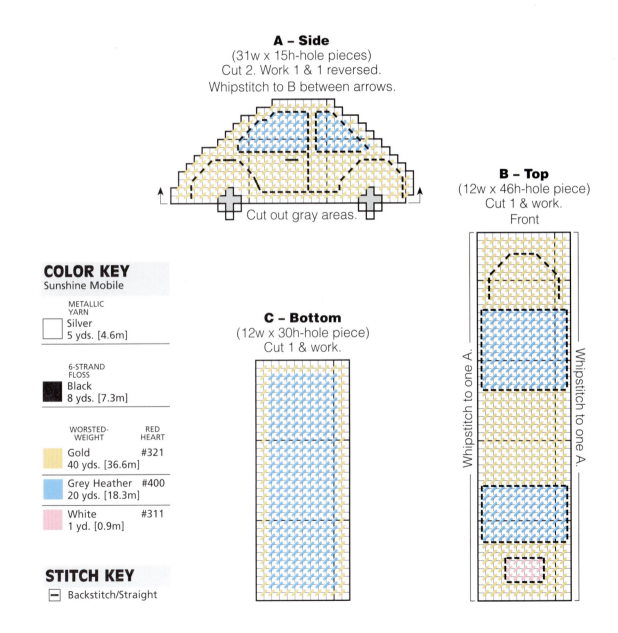

A – Side
(31w x 15h-hole pieces)
Cut 2. Work 1 & 1 reversed.
Whipstitch to B between arrows.

Cut out gray areas.

B – Top
(12w x 46h-hole piece)
Cut 1 & work.
Front

Whipstitch to one A.

Whipstitch to one A.

C – Bottom
(12w x 30h-hole piece)
Cut 1 & work.

COLOR KEY
Sunshine Mobile

	METALLIC YARN	
	Silver	
	5 yds. [4.6m]	

	6-STRAND FLOSS	
■	Black	
	8 yds. [7.3m]	

	WORSTED-WEIGHT	RED HEART
	Gold	#321
	40 yds. [36.6m]	
	Grey Heather	#400
	20 yds. [18.3m]	
	White	#311
	1 yd. [0.9m]	

STITCH KEY

⊟ Backstitch/Straight

Ready, Set, Stitch

*Get ready to stitch like a pro
with these simple, step-by-step guidelines.*

GETTING STARTED

Most plastic canvas stitchers love getting their projects organized before they even step out the door in search of supplies. A few moments of careful planning can make the creation of your project even more fun.

First of all, prepare your work area. You will need a flat surface for cutting and assembly, and you will need a place to store your materials. Good lighting is essential, and a comfortable chair will make your stitching time even more enjoyable.

Do you plan to make one project, or will you be making several of the same item? A materials list appears at the beginning of each pattern. If you plan to make several of the same item, multiply your materials accordingly. Your shopping list is ready.

CHOOSING CANVAS

Most projects can be made using standard-size sheets of canvas. Standard size sheets of 7-mesh (7 holes per inch) are always 70 x 90 holes and are about 10½" x 13½" [26.7cm x 34.3cm]. For larger projects, 7-mesh canvas also comes in 12" x 18" [30.5cm x 45.7cm], which is always 80 x 120 holes and 13½" x 22½" [34.3cm x 57.2cm], which is always 90 x 150 holes. Other shapes are available in 7-mesh, including circles, diamonds, purse forms and ovals.

10-mesh canvas (10 holes per inch) comes only in standard-size sheets, which vary slightly depending on brand. They are 10½" x 13½" [26.7cm x 34.3cm], which is always 106 x 136 holes or 11" x 14" [27.9cm x 35.6cm], which is always 108 x 138 holes.

5-mesh canvas (5 holes per inch) and 14-mesh (14 holes per inch) sheets are also available.

Some canvas is soft and pliable, while other canvas is stiffer and more rigid. To prevent canvas from cracking during or after stitching, you'll want to choose pliable canvas for projects that require shaping, like round baskets with curved handles. For easier shaping, warm canvas pieces with a blow-dry hair dryer to soften; dip in cool water to set. If your project is a box or an item that will stand alone, stiffer canvas is more suitable.

Both 7- and 10-mesh canvas sheets are available in a rainbow of colors. Most designs can be stitched on colored as well as clear canvas. When a pattern does not specify color in the materials list, you can assume clear canvas was used in the photographed model. If you'd like to stitch only a portion of the design, leaving a portion unstitched, use colored canvas to coordinate with yarn colors.

Buy the same brand of canvas for each entire project. Different brands of canvas may differ slightly in the distance between each bar.

MARKING & COUNTING TOOLS

To avoid wasting canvas, careful cutting of each piece is important. For some pieces with square corners, you might be comfortable cutting the canvas without marking it beforehand. But for pieces with lots of angles and cutouts, you may want to mark your canvas before cutting.

Always count before you mark and cut. To count holes on the graphs, look for the bolder lines showing each ten holes. These ten-count lines begin in the lower left-hand corner of each graph and are on the graph to make counting easier. To count holes on the canvas, you may use your tapestry needle, a toothpick or a plastic hair roller pick. Insert the needle or pick slightly in each hole as you count.

Most stitchers have tried a variety of marking tools and have settled on a favorite, which may be crayon, permanent marker, grease pencil or ball point pen. One of the best marking tools is a fine-point overhead projection marker, available at office supply stores. The ink is dark and easy to see and washes off completely with water. After cutting and before stitching, it's important to remove all marks so they won't stain yarn as you stitch or show through stitches later. Cloth and paper toweling removes grease pencil and crayon marks, as do fabric softener sheets that have already been used in your dryer.

CUTTING TOOLS

You may find it helpful to have several tools on hand for cutting canvas. When cutting long, straight sections, scissors, craft cutters or kitchen shears are the fastest and easiest to use. For cutting out detailed areas and trimming nubs, you may like using manicure scissors or nail clippers. If you prefer laying your canvas flat when cutting, try a craft knife and cutting surface – self-healing mats designed for sewing and kitchen cutting boards work well.

STITCHING MATERIALS

You may choose two-ply nylon plastic canvas yarn or four-ply worsted-weight yarn for stitching on 7-mesh canvas. There are about 42 yards per ounce of plastic canvas yarn and 50 yards per ounce of worsted-weight yarn.

Worsted-weight yarn is widely available and comes in wool, acrylic, cotton and blends. If you decide to use worsted-weight yarn, choose 100% acrylic for best coverage. Select worsted-weight yarn by color instead of the color names or numbers found in the Color Keys. Projects stitched with worsted-weight yarn often "fuzz" after use. "Fuzz" can be removed by shaving it off with a  fabric shaver to make your project look new again.

Plastic canvas yarn comes in about 60 colors and is a favorite of many plastic canvas designers. These yarns "wear" well both while stitching and in the finished product. When buying plastic canvas yarn, shop using the color names or numbers found in the Color Keys, or select colors of your choice.

To cover 5-mesh canvas, use a doubled strand of worsted-weight or plastic canvas yarn.

Choose sport-weight yarn or #3 pearl cotton for stitching on 10-mesh canvas. To cover 10-mesh canvas using six-strand embroidery floss, use 12 strands held together. Single and double plies of yarn will also cover 10-mesh and can be used for embroidery or accent stitching worked over needlepoint stitches – simply separate worsted-weight yarn into 2-ply or plastic canvas yarn into 1-ply. Nylon plastic canvas yarn does not perform as well as knitting worsted when separated and can be frustrating to use, but it is possible. Just use short lengths, separate into single plies and twist each ply slightly.

Embroidery floss or #5 pearl cotton can also be used for embroidery, and each covers 14-mesh canvas well.

Metallic cord is a tightly-woven cord that comes in dozens of glittering colors. Some are solid-color metallics, including gold and silver, and some have colors interwoven with gold or silver threads. If your metallic cord has a white core, the core may be removed for super-easy stitching. To do so, cut a length of cord; grasp center core fibers with tweezers or fingertips and pull. Core slips out easily. Though the sparkly look of metallics will add much to your project, you may substitute contrasting colors of yarn.

Natural and synthetic raffia straw will cover 7-mesh canvas if flattened before stitching. Use short lengths to prevent splitting, and glue ends to prevent unraveling.

CUTTING CANVAS

Follow all Cutting Instructions, Notes and labels above graphs to cut canvas. Each piece is labeled with a letter of the alphabet. Square-sided pieces are cut according to hole count, and some may not have a graph.

Unlike sewing patterns, graphs are not designed to be used as actual patterns but rather as counting, cutting and stitching guides. Therefore, graphs may not be actual size. Count the holes on the graph (see Marking & Counting Tools), mark your canvas to match, then cut. The old carpenters' adage – "Measure twice, cut once" – is good advice. Trim off the nubs close to the bar, and trim all corners diagonally.

For large projects, as you cut each piece, it is a good idea to label it with its letter and name. Use sticky labels, or fasten scrap paper notes through the canvas with a twist tie or a quick stitch with a scrap of yarn. To stay organized, you many want to store corresponding pieces together in zip-close bags.

If you want to make several of a favorite design to give as gifts or sell at bazaars, make cutting canvas easier and faster by making a master pattern. From colored canvas, cut out one of each piece required. For duplicates, place the colored canvas on top of clear canvas and cut out. If needed, secure the canvas pieces together with paper fasteners, twist ties or yarn. By using this method, you only have to count from the graphs once.

If you accidentally cut or tear a bar or two on your canvas, don't worry! Boo-boos can usually be repaired in one of several ways: heat the tip of a metal skewer and melt the canvas back together; glue torn bars with a tiny drop of craft glue, super glue or hot glue; or reinforce the torn section with a separate piece of canvas placed at the back of your work. When reinforcing with extra canvas, stitch through both thicknesses.

SUPPLIES

Yarn, canvas, needles, cutters and most other supplies needed to complete the projects in this book are available at craft and needlework stores and through mail order catalogs. Other supplies are available at fabric, hardware and discount stores.

NEEDLES & OTHER STITCHING TOOLS

Blunt-end tapestry needles are used for stitching plastic canvas. Choose a No. 16 needle for stitching 5- and 7-mesh, a No. 18 for stitching 10-mesh and a No. 24 for stitching 14-mesh canvas. A small pair of embroidery scissors for snipping yarn is handy. Try using needle-nosed jewelry pliers for pulling the needle through several thicknesses of canvas and out of tight spots too small for your hand.

STITCHING THE CANVAS

Stitching Instructions for each section are found after the Cutting Instructions. First, refer to the illustrations of basic stitches found on page 159 to familiarize yourself with the stitches used. Illustrations will be found near the graphs for pieces worked using special stitches. Follow the numbers on the tiny graph beside the illustration to make

each stitch – bring your needle up from the back of the work on odd numbers and down through the front of the work on the even numbers.

Before beginning, read the Stitching Instructions to get an overview of what you'll be doing. You'll find that some pieces are stitched using colors and stitches indicated on graphs, and for other pieces you will be given a color and stitch to use to cover the entire piece.

Cut yarn lengths between 18" [45.7cm] to 36" [91.4cm]. Thread needle; do not tie a knot in the end. Bring your needle up through the canvas from the back, leaving a short length of yarn on the wrong side of the canvas. As you begin to stitch, work over this short length of yarn. If you are beginning with Continental Stitches, leave a 1" [2.5cm] length, but if you are working longer stitches, leave a longer length.

In order for graph colors to contrast well, graph colors may not match yarn colors. For instance, a light yellow may be selected to represent the metallic cord color gold, or a light blue may represent white yarn.

When following a graph showing several colors,

you may want to work all the stitches of one color at the same time. Some stitchers prefer to work with several colors at once by threading each on a separate needle and letting the yarn not being used hang on the wrong side of the work. Either way, remember that strands of yarn run across the wrong side of the work may show through the stitches from the front.

As you stitch, try to maintain an even tension on the yarn. Loose stitches will look uneven, and tight stitches will let the canvas show through. If your yarn twists as you work, you may want to let your needle and yarn hang and untwist occasionally.

When you end a section of stitching or finish a thread, weave the yarn through the back side of your last few stitches; then trim it off.

CONSTRUCTION & ASSEMBLY

After all pieces of an item needing assembly are stitched, you will find the order of assembly is listed in the Stitching Instructions and sometimes illustrated in Diagrams found with the graphs. For best results, join pieces in the order written. Refer to the Stitch Key and to the directives near the graphs for precise attachments.

FINISHING TIPS

To combat glue strings when using a hot glue gun, practice a swirling motion as you work. After placing the drop of glue on your work, lift the gun slightly and swirl to break the stream of glue, as if you were making an ice cream cone. Have a cup of water handy when gluing. For those times that you'll need to touch the glue, first dip your finger into the water just enough to dampen it. This will minimize the glue sticking to your finger, and it will cool and set the glue more quickly.

To attach beads, use a bit more glue to form a cup around the bead. If too much shows after drying, use a craft knife to trim off excess glue.

Scotchguard® or other fabric protectors may be used on your finished projects. However, avoid using a permanent marker if you plan to use a fabric protector, and be sure to remove all other markings before stitching. Fabric protectors can cause markings to bleed, staining yarn.

FOR MORE INFORMATION

Sometimes even the most experienced needlecrafters can find themselves having trouble following instructions. If you have difficulty completing your project, write to Plastic Canvas Editors, The Needlecraft Shop, 23 Old Pecan Road, Big Sandy, Texas 75755 (903) 636-4000 or (800) 259-4000, www.needlecraftshop.com.

Stitch Guide

Backstitch
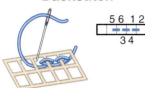

French Knot

Sheaf Stitch

Continental
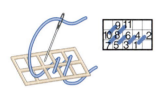

Lazy Daisy Stitch

Smyrna Small T-Over

Continental Reverse
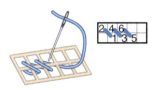

Long Over Three Bars
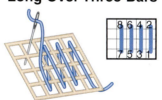

Smyrna Large T-Over
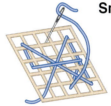

Cross

Modified Turkey Work

Straight

Diagonal Horizontal
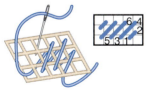

Overcast

Whipstitch

Diagonal Reverse Horizontal
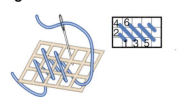

Scotch Over Three Bars

Bead Attachment

Pattern Index

Designer Index